Tamar's Closet

A Journey of Healing

LAURIE A. MALLIETT

WestBow
PRESS
A DIVISION OF THOMAS NELSON

WestBow Press books may be ordered through booksellers or by contacting:

WestBow Press
A Division of Thomas Nelson
1663 Liberty Drive
Bloomington, IN 47403
www.westbowpress.com
1 (866) 928-1240

Because of the dynamic nature of the Internet, any web addresses or links contained in this book may have changed since publication and may no longer be valid. The views expressed in this work are solely those of the author and do not necessarily reflect the views of the publisher, and the publisher hereby disclaims any responsibility for them.

Any people depicted in stock imagery provided by Thinkstock are models, and such images are being used for illustrative purposes only.
Certain stock imagery © Thinkstock.

ISBN: 978-1-4908-1006-5 (sc)
ISBN: 978-1-4908-1005-8 (e)

Library of Congress Control Number: 2013917504

Printed in the United States of America.

WestBow Press rev. date: 10/11/2013

Table of Contents

Foreword

Truth is a very powerful thing. Truth has revealed the laws of nature, unraveled mysteries, impeached presidents, dispensed justice, brought down Fortune 500 companies and righted wrongs. But truth is also liberating. The bible says in John 8:32 that, 'You shall know the truth and the truth will make you free.'

We have often said that truth will set you free, but that quote is wrong. The truth makes you free. What's the difference? To 'set' something free is to do it immediately, but to 'make' something free is a process. If something is made free then it has gone through the process of not only being free externally, but also being free internally. You can be set free from a moment, but if the emotions of that moment have not been dealt with then you will never truly be free.

In this book, "Tamar's Closet," the author begins to examine the process that is needed to allow someone to truly be free. It is not an immediate process and does not happen overnight, but if time, patience, support and truth are applied, then you can be free. Free doesn't mean that the occurrence is erased from the DNA of your experience, but it does mean that it no longer binds you and restricts your growth and momentum as a valued, treasured and beautiful human being.

The bible also says in Revelation 12:11 'And they overcame . . . by the word of their testimony.' It is rare that you find someone who is willing to share the pain of their past and their journey to healing in such a transparent way, but this is exactly what Laurie Malliett has done. Just as truth is liberating, silence is debilitating. Silence to the witness of being mishandled by others and silence of the journey of healing from being mishandled is equally as tragic. The only way to begin to dispel the darkness is by shedding light. And it is in the shedding of light, as painful as it may be, that actually begins to allow others who have shared experiences to overcome.

The central message of this book is that you are worth it. You are worth going through this process to bring the beginning of healing to your mind, emotions and life. In the words of John 10:10, it's time for you 'to have LIFE and have it in abundance.'

Jason Turner, Th.D.
Associate Pastor
President and Interim Dean
Dominion Bible College

Acknowledgments

It was almost six years that God put it into my heart to write this book. I have found growth and healing from doing just that. He has blessed me with the insight that can only come from Him. Thank you Father God for your enduring love and compassion towards me.

I wish to thank my mom for being there as a support, teaching me to help and love others. Her time as a foster parent taught me to give to community. We need each other.

Thanking always my sisters and friends who have prayed for and encouraged me thru this process of writing.

I wish to show appreciation to my husband who has graciously allowed part of our lives to be shared with you for your growth and healing. He has been supportive of this book from its inception. His growth in the Lord is proof that God heals and restores.

Thank you to my Writers Club, for their guidance and helpful advice. Judi Ess for her friendship and help with editing.

Prologue

Our clothes closets reveal what we want others to think of us, how we think of ourselves and much more. They reveal things about us that our best friends may never know. Together we will be digging into our closets, revealing our true identity, and correcting our poor self-image. We will learn better choices for ourselves as we learn our true value as **women of great excellence**.

Although there are many books out there to assist us in our healing process, this one is unlike any other you will read. It will reveal integral parts of ourselves *as* we reflect on our choices and inner thoughts about ourselves. It's my sole purpose to write this book to you, my sisters, who have endured suffering at the hands of someone else, for your self-worth and healing.

One thing I need to mention is that on this journey, you are opening up the Pandora's Box of your past experiences and you *will* experience pain in the process. It cannot be helped. PTSD, post-traumatic stress disorder, is normal for most victims of abuse. We may have tried hard to believe it is all over and it never affects us anymore. On the contrary, we know it is still there and we will have trigger points and emotional responses that may or may not be healthy. If we are honest with ourselves, our responses are sometimes mismatched with the situation. We may have, at times, offended others by our lack of restraint of words and emotions poured out on someone who may not deserve it. If we are not careful, we may become someone who abuses others unknowingly, due our painful past. We certainly don't want to do that!

This book is not meant to replace counseling. I had outbursts of anger and resentment, uncontrollable weeping, frustrations and a lot of self-doubt for months while working through some of my pain. This is where counseling can be of great value to you. I myself went to an abuse shelter for classes and found help there. For more information on counseling see Appendix. It was through their painting classes that I was able to unleash the start of my process of healing and letting go. It is said that if you just have one person who believes in you, you can do anything! I do believe that is true. I had a few people believe in me and it definitely helped me to change the way I looked at myself. Case in point: *I am writing* this book for you!

Please, let your friends, family and others close to you know that you are starting a journey of healing. It will help them to understand when you are overly emotional or angry. It is nothing to be ashamed of, it's a natural response to opening up our mind and pent up emotions, which hold painful memories. *The pain needs to come up* to the front to be addressed. Don't stop the process when it does get painful and confusing. Work through it to overcome the past lies and *start believing the truth* that you are marvelously made by God. You are not alone.

Maybe, after your journey through this book, you may think of others who have also suffered and can recommend this book and share your story with them as well. We need each other and do better if we have the love and support of others during our process of healing.

Come and join me by taking the journey as we uncover truths and the lies we believed. Let's learn who *we really are, women of excellence, of great value and honor. You are a gift <u>from</u> God—<u>to</u> the world.* This is a unique process of spiritual and emotional enlightenment. I have thought much about you and prayed for your healing. Know that you are greatly loved and highly valued. I believe in you. You are never alone.

Your sister,
Laurie

I have the privilege of knowing the Lord Jesus Christ as my personal savior. He has promised never to leave nor forsake me no matter what. Even as I accused Him of allowing the bad things to happen to me, He was still there. He is a big God and can handle anything I give Him.

I use the story of Tamar and other scriptures to assist us in our new self-worth. The Word of God, the Bible, has been a comfort to me in very hard times. I hope you find that to be true as well. As you read the words in the Bible, see what benefits await you. Be brave and try new things.

If you are reading this book because you know someone who was traumatized, I am so very proud of you. Most women don't get the support they need. You will make a great friend, spouse, support system for someone who needs healing. Please refrain from telling them to get over it, or move on. If they are in pain, *pray with* them, *pray for* them and if they will allow you to, hold them. Tell them they are loved; express your positive concern for them. Don't leave them alone to wonder if anyone cares. Get involved, whatever we do to the least of these, we do to Christ. Would you abandon Him? I didn't think so.

Introduction
Including Journaling and purging pages

The journal pages are for you to write down your thoughts, questions and anything you learned from each chapter. Some journal and purging pages will ask you to go through your closet of emotions and your actual closet of clothes. For this book to benefit you the way it was initially intended, I recommend you take the time to read one chapter at a time and take time to let it sink in. Then, use the journal pages before going to next chapter. You will also benefit from writing down your feelings and the truths you learned. Working through our closet and emotional attachments to our belongings will bring clarity in our lives. Dating your entries will give you a good timeline of emotional growth.

The purging pages may include a specific clothing item for you to consider. It isn't meant to suggest you have every piece of clothing mentioned, just an analogy of garments. It is my prayer for you to have healing in your heart, mind and soul. You will hopefully find this freeing and eye opening as you take a real good look at your wardrobe. This metaphor on closets and clothes stems from my love of fashion and my heart for women to be healed from past painful experiences.

There are chapters on spiritual garments towards the back for those of you who want to know more about the spiritual life of a believer.

Tamar's Story

In our emotional closets, we have many stories to tell of events that have changed the way we see ourselves. Unfortunately, our memories are attached to either really good or really bad memories. Our emotional state always reflects our physical state, and vise-versa. Tamar was one of the virgin daughters of King David. You may not know who she is now, but her story is in the Bible for a purpose. As her story unfolds, we are privy to her deepest sorrows and painful life experiences. Many of us share those same awful experiences. However, it is my prayer that we do not follow her footsteps of desolation. Tamar's story is found in the Old Testament. Let's read the brief account taken from the King James Version:

2 Samuel, Chapter 13, verses 1-20

"Amnon, the son of David, had a lovely sister, whose name was Tamar, and he loved her. Amnon was so distressed over his sister that he became sick: for she was a virgin. And it was improper for Amnon to do anything to her Then Amnon pretended to be ill: When the king came to see him, Amnon said to the king, 'Please let Tamar my sister come and make a couple of cakes for me in my sight that I may eat from her hand.' And David sent home to Tamar saying, 'Now go to your brother Amnon's house, and prepare food for him.'

So Tamar went to her brother Amnon's house and he was lying down. Then she made cakes in his sight and baked them. And she took the pan and placed them out before him, but he refused to eat. Then Amnon said, 'Have everyone go out from me.' And they wall went out from him. Then Amnon said to Tamar, 'Bring the food into the bedroom that I may eat from your hand.' And Tamar took the cakes, which she had made and brought them to Amnon her brother in the bedroom

Now, when she had brought them to him to eat he took hold of her and said to her, 'Come lie with me, my sister.' And she answered him, 'No my brother, do not force me, for no such thing should be done in Israel. Do not do this disgraceful thing! And I, where could I take my shame? And as for you, you would be like one of the fools in Israel. Now therefore, please speak to the king: for he will not withhold me from you.' However, he would not heed her voice and being stronger than she, he forced her and lay with her.

Then Amnon hated her exceedingly, so that he the hatred with which he hated her was g greater than the love with which he had loved her. And Amnon said to her, 'Arise, be gone!' And she said to him, 'No, indeed! This evil of sending me away is worse than the other that you did to me.' But he would not listen to her. Then he called his servant who attended him, and said, 'Here! Put this woman out, away from me, and bolt the door behind her.' And his servant put her out and bolted the door behind her. Then Tamar put ashes on her head and went away crying bitterly. And Absalom her brother said to her, 'Has Amnon your brother been with you? But now hold your peace, my sister. He is your brother; do not take this thing to heart.' So Tamar remained *desolate* in her brother Absalom's house."

Well, there you have it. A recorded incident of sexual abuse in the Bible. Ever wonder why it was recorded and printed for all to see? I think it is so we can learn from it. Today we would call what happened to Tamar, incest. It happens more than is told, unfortunately. We do find out, later on, that Tamar's brother Absalom takes vengeance on his half-brother and has him murdered.

Deuteronomy 2:28, 29
"If a man find a damsel *that is* a virgin,
which is not betrothed, and lay hold on her, and lie with her, and they be found;
Then the man that lay with her shall give unto the damsel's father
fifty *shekels* of silver, and she shall be his wife;
because he hath humbled her, he may not put her away all his days."

This scripture explains why she told Amnon to ask her father for her to marry him. It was better to marry her than to use her for sex and shame her in that way. Please don't misunderstand me here, I don't think you should marry your abuser. Oh no! That would bring a lot of other trauma and problems to your relationship. If you have already, I pray God will help you get through your relationship with counseling and healing.

What happened to Tamar was a devastating blow to her self-image, because of the society in which she lived. Think of all the rumors that went across the land about her. I know people who never married due to the abuse that happened to them. Broken trust and painful memories keep us from the freedom to be whole and fulfilled. We become self-protecting. We do not want to allow ourselves to be put in any type of situation like that again. It is my prayer that as you work through this book, you will not follow her path of desolation.

Be courageous to do the work of finding the truth. Let the truths you learn be the new steps on the path to a fuller, richer life. The one you were destined to have. Yes, there is fun, freedom, life, and joy and love for you in this world. Begin with Christ and let him direct your path to each of those things, thus fulfilling your destiny. It encompasses so much more than you can imagine. It isn't too late for you. Come with me and see on this our journey what is all-available to you. Begin to trust in small ways. Even if you have to do it afraid, courage is just that, doing things while you are still afraid. Our journey awaits, let's do this together.

Journal page for chapter one, Tamar's Story

On this page, I would like you to focus on what Tamar's story means to you. How does her story stir you?

Closets

We all have closets and stuff them with an abundance of items. Whether or not you have an elite walk-in room with coveted shelving and drawers, or you are limited to a simple small rack to hang your clothes, it is still a storage place. Let me explain. When we think of storage, we think of things we rarely use or do not want others to see.

I chose to title this book, Tamar's Closet, for several reasons. We can all relate to a closet and many of us can relate to Tamar who found herself in a sexually abusive situation.

In the process of my healing, the Lord has shown me many things about myself. My past is still in mourning and my closet is one of the most "telling" things about me. You may never see all that I have, or have had, in my closet, but the "stuff" I have in there tells a lot about me. It would, if you paid attention closely, tell you about my decisions, or choices I have made. It might say what I wish others see me as. It might not tell you everything, but you would definitely see a lot of "me."

You would notice I love shoes, not a difficult observation, haa haa, I have several boxes of shoes. To me, shoes should match the outfit and my mood. And, admittedly, sometimes I can be moody, yes, even me. I pay more attention to the shoes rather than the purse, unlike my daughter who loves purses. Not to say purses do not matter, they do, but for me they are more of an accessory than the actual outfit. I am a multi-faceted person, so you would see a variety of clothes. I like many things from camping and hiking to dressing up and intelligent conversation. I love to create, invent and one day I will learn to build things too.

The Early Years

Let me tell you a little about myself and my "closet" of stuff. I was the second born of five children in a Catholic family. I was sexually molested at an early age. I was not the only one my abuser molested. I have had nightmares from it as well. I was so young I really did not know what was all happening and I was powerless to do anything about it. I still carry guilt with me like it is all my fault.

My father died at the age of thirty unexpectedly. I was nine years old. I tried to live a good religious life in the Catholic faith. Oh, I believed there was a God, but I had no idea He wanted a personal relationship with me. I was a tomboy growing up due to my past abuse. I was more comfortable around others, especially boys or men, acting like one of them. I felt I would not be noticed as female and I wouldn't be in any danger of misuse. Well, that only worked so long due to puberty.

I was so insecure I sucked my thumb until I was in 7th grade. I was extremely shy, so much so that I was afraid to ask to go to the bathroom. My 7th grade math teacher when counting heads, numbered me as ½, because I was so small. I was a wall flower. I was not popular, nor did I exceed in much of anything, I just tried to get through life the best I could. I didn't have any direction. I had hobbies, but not a lot of guidance or support.

Tumultuous Teen Years

By the time I was in senior high I didn't get "the bird and the bees talk," so I didn't know that any type of touching before marriage is not good. I knew I didn't want sex but assumed fondling is what is required of one when you date. I was usually dumped since I wouldn't have sex with any of the boys I dated. I had teachers who were always staring at my chest. One even said I looked like a playboy bunny. It made me feel very uncomfortable and targeted. Nothing ever came of those situations thankfully. I never allowed myself to be alone with anyone. One Sunday, after leaving the Catholic Church service, the Lord spoke to me and said, "There is more to *Me* than this." Shortly thereafter, a friend invited me to her Nazarene Church. I learned what it meant to have a relationship with Christ. I attended church often and found solace in the friendships and in serving and learning about the Lord.

Still in high school, I loved tennis and one neighbor's father asked me to play tennis with him at the school. I never thought it was bad and so I did. Afterwards, he told me he had a nickname for me, Lily. I found out it meant, "Laurie, I love you." I was freaked out. I didn't know where to go with that so I ignored him.

While doing my mom's errands, I had to give his wife something from my mom. I hesitated, but what would I say? He asked if I was going to go to church and I said yes. While his wife was there, he said he'd pick me up and I said "No, I would not need a ride," but she insisted. What was I going to say? I was still so shy. He did pick me up and we attended church. He wanted to stop afterward and get a soda and I said okay, only so I could muster up the courage to tell him to stay away from me. I never got the chance and when he drove me home, he said he loved me again and I said it was adultery. He disagreed believe it or not. I wanted to open the door and roll out but my hand wouldn't open the door. He did take me home, thankfully. Even though I was physically unharmed, I had nightmares for three months of being kidnapped and raped. Although, in the dreams, I woke before the actual act of rape.

I went to school in fear of being kidnapped on the way there. He actually had the gall to write me love letters. I took them to my pastor, who called the man and told him to stay away. The man still wrote one more time 3 months later to see if I wanted to come and clean his apartment. I felt like a home wrecker and I didn't even do anything wrong. Of course, I didn't answer his letter and again gave it to my pastor. He called the man and again told him to stay away. Actually, I don't know why the police were not called. I was under the age of eighteen.

Graduation to degradation

I was a very lonely confused girl by the time I graduated from high school. I had friends but the Christian ones were not that close to me. I didn't fit in anywhere in my mind. I was tempted to join the Army and prove myself and become tough. I was also tempted to become a stripper since the only type of attention I did receive was that from other's sexual desires. I could rationalize in my mind at least I'd be wanted. I did think about becoming a nun so I didn't have to deal with evil men and feel protected in the church. Well, much thanks to other's prayers I am sure, I didn't do any of those three things. I really didn't want to be a nun, I really did want a family. As a believer, I knew the stripper life was not for me. I may have felt I wanted attention but it would not be for the right reasons. I really didn't want to become a victim again, nor did I want to become something someone owned. And well, I guess, I wasn't that strong emotionally to go and join the military.

I dated someone from the church and even though he wasn't a born again Christian, we were engaged to be married. I realized I had prayed "Lord, let this be your will." Then I prayed "Your will be done," and put out a fleece. (A fleece is something you ask God for that only He can do to show you His direction in a situation) God answered with a no and I was dumped. Four months later, I was back with the person. I used my own thinking: God will bring him into salvation. Thinking in my own mind, that was why God said no to me. He did have a belief in God, he just didn't live for God. We got married and within three months I was already being verbally and physically abused. There were moments I was afraid for my life. I was tormented by his knife throwing, thankfully not at me. He would destroy mine or his possessions in front of me. My new marriage was in trouble. I cried myself to sleep for a week and prayed and God helped me to get through it. I didn't tell anyone at that time. I always thought I had no value. I reasoned that if I did have ANY value, I would be treated with more respect. I rationalized that since that didn't happen, I didn't have any value. Others did to me what they wanted to and I had to just deal with it.

Baby Blessings

I had two miscarriages within the first year, six months apart. Three months after the second miscarriage I prayed for twins and God granted me my first two girls. Still the verbal abuse and then the sexual abuse. Even though I said no, he did it anyway. I cried all through it. I felt that I had no say in the matter, which further insulted me like when I was abused as a young child.

Another miscarriage and another daughter born. He was still abusive and resentment started in me. Such anger in my home and I tried so very hard to make it happy. After being married 10 years, I realized that I hated him. One day, during the mealtime, he yelled at the girls over nothing. I got so mad that I yelled at him to stop it. I couldn't even eat, I was so nauseous from the yelling. He got mad but I didn't want the girls to think that was normal healthy family life. It was wrong and I couldn't stand it anymore.

My husband put up quite the good guy show at church. It was hard for me to get anyone to listen to me. We attended churches, which had no real training for spousal abuse. I continued in my anger and pain. Being pushed away emotionally and many other ways, I turned to God for help, asking Him to help me to get through the pain of loneliness and help our marriage. I focused on relationships with my friends and being a mother. It wasn't long before I was lonely again and I turned to another man for comfort. Friends that close don't always stay friends. I fell in love and realized I couldn't remain friends anymore. I didn't want to be an adulterer, no matter how lonely I felt. Even though there wasn't any sexual act, my heart was gone. I decided to stay in the marriage, after all, I made vows before God. So I terminated the friendship. That was very hard to let go of someone that I thought was what I wanted.

Trauma Drama

Neither of us understood the effects of PTSD on a Viet Nam Vet, which he was. Nor of the PTSD of a victim of childhood sexual abuse, which I was. Goodness, looking back, it's quite amazing we are still married. My husband still had a lot of anger and more abusive actions. I got smacked in the face and head twice and you could hear my vertebrae crack down my neck. I thought of suicide a few times, but since I was a mother, I couldn't do that to my kids. I loved them and tried giving them the best I had, even in those abusive times. We weren't abused all the time, but we were never sure when and how bad it was going to be. Always waiting for the shoe to drop. Always wondering and feeling the air of what was next when he came home from work. It was so tense you could feel it. It felt like I could never relax and rely on my spouse.

Years went on with more mean idle words, unkind attitudes and very selfish behavior. I was married but felt all alone. Trapped with nowhere to turn but God. I had nightmares of people coming to tell me he had died. I guess it was my subconscious telling me I couldn't handle it anymore. I started getting angry before he did and standing up to him. I threatened divorce, but with the kids, I knew I couldn't afford to care for them like I wanted on my own. He had, during those days, never apologized for any of the actions he did. He always justified them and blamed me for making him mad. He actually never physically abused the kids, but verbal yelling is still abusive and can be more damaging to the soul. He lied often to get his way and to avoid conversations with me on several topics. I thought he was having an affair, because he would reject me often. I didn't know marriage would be so lonely. I prayed to God asking Him for help in the marriage and every time I did, it seemed to be a bit better, less arguing and a bit more livable. Reading the Bible got me through all this with my mind intact.

When I was sick with pneumonia, he was mad that I wouldn't go to church and help him with the girls. Just when I was about to pass out I grabbed onto his shirt. He yelled at me and threw my hand off, saying "GET OFF ME LADY," like I was someone he didn't know. I retreated to the powder room and he followed and continued yelling at me until I couldn't hear anything anymore. My head was just ringing. So he took the kids to his mom's. I was so sick all I could do was lie in the bed and barely make it to the bathroom. I was too weak to get myself anything, since everything was downstairs. He would come home to feed himself lunch and never feed me or make sure I was taken care of. I started crying but I realized I couldn't breathe due to the pneumonia so I had to stop. The Lord sent one of my neighbors to come help me one day and I was truly blessed. Since my dad had died at age 30 with complications of pneumonia, I got a bit scared.

When I found a lump in my breast, I was afraid. I had made an appointment for a mammogram. The night before I went in, I said to myself, give him another chance, this is serious. So I went up to talk to him, it was only 5-10 min after he went up for bed. He yelled at me for nearly two hours for knowing better than to wake him up. If I took a bath or shower after he went to bed, I would get yelled at because he could hear the water running.

A Reprieve

We moved and my mom came to stay with us. Unknowingly to me, they decided to throw a surprise birthday party for me. That in itself was unusual. He told me to get into the car. We drove a bit and he seemed casual, but I was afraid. He drove by the lake and into wooded areas I was unfamiliar with and then back towards home. I admitted to him that I was afraid and that I thought he was going to hurt me. His response was

"Maybe a year ago I would have." That was no solace for me I'll tell you. Things were better while she was living with us. But when my mom left after 7 months, he started the bad behavior again. This time calling me bad names and being really mean.

We moved again and got into a good church and I found a friend who prayed for me. I mean really prayed for me. God woke her up one night, just to tell her to pray for me. I was tempted to go into a bar and I did not drink. I felt so very thirsty all of a sudden, and I did not care what would happen next. She prayed and I was able to resist the enemy. I prayed and cried often. I had to cry quietly because, in the first three months of my marriage if I did cry in front of him, he get angry and would grab me by my arms and shake me. I had bruises from those times.

For about three years, every six months, I would cry for hours I would be so sad I could not help it. I just couldn't do it anymore. God always gave me the strength to go on and do what I needed to just keep on some more.

I hated anniversaries and Valentines Days. I didn't love him and didn't trust him. How do you put that into a card? So I avoided mushy cards and tried to focus on the "future" in those days.

Admitting I needed help

After 17 years of living like this, I became very emotional. I went to a shelter for abused women for some guidance and support. The church I had been in was not helpful and I couldn't afford professional counseling. I knew I needed help to get through my past so I could be a better mother to my kids. The women at the shelter were very supportive. They helped me to understand what abuse is and how to handle life better and make better life affirming choices. I *do* matter, and I *do* have value. That only made me angrier because I wasn't *treated* that way. I had to learn to control my anger with my spouse. I gave God one more year to work on the marriage. I couldn't live like that anymore; it felt more like I was dying. I wanted out of the lonely marriage and I wanted to be loved, not rejected and left alone all the time.

I had surgery and my husband was not helpful. He sent me away for a week because he wasn't sure how to take care of me. When I crashed a moped trying to learn how to drive it and got a head injury, I got little to no help from him either. A few days after the accident I lost my short-term memory. He said he didn't think I had a memory loss problem and was unsupportive and unkind.

Strength from above

I prayed often and God gave me the grace to endure for my husband's sake. I could have left, but my husband's welfare was always on the back of my mind. I was afraid he would hurt himself. God gave me the courage to continue. My husband did finally apologize for what he knew he did, but he will never know the full extent of his behavior. God knows everything and He's helping me to change too. I am still learning to trust in the marriage. With God's help, I can do all things that God has for me. I chose to stay in the marriage, giving God all my sorrows and waiting on God to complete the work my husband needs. God has proven Himself faithful as He is doing a work in my husband both in his personal life and in our marriage. It is now an easier life, with God blessing the changes that are being made daily.

God says He will be there for me and give me whatever I need to do His will. I need to give God my will and He will protect my heart if I give it to Him. I can't stay the victim anymore. I am not just a survivor anymore, I am victorious! Victorious over the abuse, victorious over the sinner, victorious over the lies I believed about myself. *Victorious over the enemy satan's attacks to get me to sin.*

There are people in my life that had shoved the knowledge of the abuse that happened to me under the rug. Ignoring me and my pain, some even **blamed** me for revealing it for healing. It's sad, but people actually tell someone who has been abused to "get over it." Clearly they don't understand it is a lifelong process of healing and restoring God's plan for us. Why do they think that the abused will get over it just because someone was tired of hearing they have a problem?

Please, pay attention! We, as victims, *complain because we* don't know what to do and don't get the help we so desperately seek. It is a sign of where we are at. Not a conjunction for someone to tell us to shut up and move on. We need a good friend to help us get through the process of healing life's painful moments. We need life affirming hugs and love from God through people. Giving us hope, help, and showing us God's will and praying is much more enlightening. Because there is hope.

I only thought of how to get out of it to stop the pain. I should have asked for help sooner and kept looking for more help. God was and still is in control and on the Throne of Glory. God is our hope. I want you to thrive. Actually, I want you to live the life God planned for you, with Him as Lord of your life. He is there for you. I could not have the empathy for you if I had not suffered myself and come out of it with God and in God with His strengthening power over my life. When the events that happened to me occurred, no one protected me from harm, or took me to the doctor or counseling. No one defended me or put justice into action afterwards on my behalf. I had to bear it all alone, the pain, shame and blame from others. I am writing this for you, so you can realize you don't need to continue to take the blame or shame anymore. I have a really hard time watching shows that have abuse in them. Inside of me just cringes and anger rises up. I can't stand to watch it, especially when justice isn't served.

Even so, we cannot assume the position of vigilante. We need to follow the laws of our land and obey them ourselves or we are guilty of sin ourselves. Taking things in our own hands only complicates things and further destroys families. A family member who kills or harms the offender and gets put in jail is no good to the ones who needs them to care and protect them. I need to remember that God will take vengeance over my enemies, those that hurt me. He will raise my head, guide my heart and bring me peace and love.

Maybe that is why I am prone to watching romantic comedies and Cinderella stories. Love wins out in the end. Love conquers. Love is pursued and found. How beautiful is that? Isn't that what we all hope and long for? That is why abuse is so devastating, because you trust someone that maybe you love and they hurt you so deeply. You begin to question love and its consequences.

But, God has always loved YOU. His relationship is pure and without pain. For me it is the most powerful relationship I have ever experienced. He never left me. He was ever present and always FOR ME, in all of it. But there is more. Just because the abuse is no longer occurring, doesn't mean that the pain is over with. I want to offer His love, peace, and presence in your journey of healing. And it is a journey. Please take it with me. One day at a time. One moment at a time. One piece of clothing at a time. One memory at a time. Healing is ours. It has always been available. Now is the time for us to flourish.

Journal pages for chapter two, Closets

On these pages, I would like you to open up your emotional closet. You may want to journal the abuse you have experienced. It's okay to take as much time on this section as you need. Days even if necessary. Pray as you begin this process, weep when you need to. There is no rush to the healing process, only do begin it. By acknowledging the pain, the disappointments and anger it will open up your heart for freedom. Be as detailed as you want or as brief as you need. If you need to, go ahead and skip this page and come back later after you are ready to do it. This is just the beginning, it gets easier with each chapter.

Opening Closet Doors

I want to offer you a new, freer, look at the rest of your life. Tamar had to leave it all behind and lived in her other brother's home for the remaining years of her life. She never, ever, wore her beautiful princess garments again. Those garments represented her purity, honor, hope, and blessings. She felt none of those things after the abuse. There was nothing pure or honorable about how she was treated. Seldom do people give respect to one who has been mistreated. We also feel used and worthless, wanting more, but not even daring enough to keep hoping or believing we can actually have it. She remained desolate. We choose desolation also when we leave behind our dreams and hopes for a wonderful life.

I want to shout "Go back to your father's house. Go back to your position as princess. Go back and redeem your virtue and honor. Put on the princess garments and royal crown. Hold your head high. You are worthy of beauty and honor and blessings." So I say to you, you are still worthy of being loved and having a loving husband and children and a place in this life. Be it a career or position, **you were made for God's Glory** and His divine plan for *you* is magnificent.

Sadly, for her there was no hope of an ever after, because in her culture if you were not a virgin you didn't deserve to marry. There was no one recorded in the Bible who told her she could, and should, still live her dream life. Has anyone told you how worthy you actually are? Someone to be there for you to push you harder and encourage you to become something great? If you haven't had someone to be there for you, to help you through life's hard times, the best advice I can give you is to forgive them and move on. Most of them do the very best they know how and you have to release them. No sense hanging onto what will never be. They need what you need as well. It's my prayer you will learn some things and be able to pass on what you have learned and have been healed from.

That's what I am doing through this book, passing it on.

I'm encouraging you now, no, I am telling you now, "**GO back to your former unharmed Self.**" She is still there hiding under the ruins. Even ruins get cleaned up and restored, mostly by loving, patient visionaries. They see what no one else does.

One of my favorite types of shows is *Extreme Makeovers*. Change is good but it can be hard too. The contestants first have to change their behaviors and then they change the outer appearance. That is why we will be going through our closets. As we realize what these clothes mean to us and why we have chosen those styles, sizes, colors, etc., we will be changing our inside and then our outside.

We can get so very jealous of those we think are better looking or smarter than what we think we are. God created *everyone* to have a great potential for success in this world in one area or another. Remember the old adage: If you always do, what you always have done, you will always get what you have always gotten. Well, that is so true. We **must** change our thinking to go back to **our original God designed life.**

You will find the **Real You,** the one that has been hiding under all the clothes of shame, guilt, pain, the burden of unforgiveness, and unworthiness. You will feel right in the clothes you chose for your new freer self. Just give it a chance to set in and become the new you I know you can be. Not the burdened, heavy, unloved, self.

How do you find yourself? It starts with going back to your dreams and visions of what you had as a child or young woman. God first gives us the dreams and then He helps us to fulfill them. He will always enable us to do what He has planned for us to do in the first place. God is the Creator, Master Designer. The other guy, satan, is just the lowly, cowardly imitator. When we are tempted, it is from the imitator, not the dream fulfilling God. Think with me for a moment. If you had all the money you needed to hire a contractor to redo your mansion, would you;

- Choose the buildings original architect, the one who created the blueprint for the mansion and was there while it was being built.
- Hire the imitator who has big lofty words with nothing to back them up with?

If you could wear a Vera Wang wedding dress, why would you settle for going to a Goodwill store for the most important day of your life? Do you get the sense that you are undermining your potential and life by settling for shall I say, *nothing*? Nothing is what we get when we don't go for our potential or desired life. (Let me add wholesome, healthy, godly life). **You are the mansion**; God is your designer, master carpenter, masonry worker, roofer, etc. He wants to come and **live in your** place and **restore** you, His creation, to your former glory and original purpose. He wants to live in your heart, your mansion, while he begins the work to restore you.

You may resist change because you are uncomfortable in new things, but let me assure you of one thing, nothing worth having ever came easy. How we dress our **new** selves will be a very important aspect of our genuine love of self. Revealing to ourselves and others our maturity and growth in the Lord. We will be demonstrating the power of the Holy Spirit from God for our healing. As we grow more in confidence, we will know who we are in Christ and what **our inheritance in the Lord** as believers is.

Push through the pain and come over to the other side. No one can erase what has happened to us, but we can endure and seek hope from God. After we have found it, we can share it with others in our lives and around the world. Journeys take us through many areas of our lives that require strength and courage. They're all different for everyone so don't judge yours by comparison. We all need to take the pilgrimage for ourselves. It is between us and our designer, God, to do the work and restoration needed to create the re-make of our lives. Who doesn't want a make-over? Go ahead and seek godly counsel and women who have done the work and know the process of healing. Seek out the encouragement from other's success stories. Though ultimately, it is a journey you make *towards* God and His inheritance for you and your future with Him.

This life is just a shadow of what is to come. Walk with me, my sister, and see for yourself the wonders of the Lord as you open your heart, life, "closet of pain" and closet of your wardrobe to Him. Releasing everything to Him, your pain, past, sin, unforgiveness, everything to Him and your anger too. After you've given all that to Him, *He will prove to you what He can do for you.* He has perfect timing and His will is a perfect fit for you. He has plans for your best life from here on out. What's not to love about someone who loves you that much? Can you, will you, trust Him to be there for you? You have nothing to lose if you try His plan. I pray you can open your closet doors to His plans and your heart to His Holy Spirit leading.

Closet purging time for, Opening Closet Doors

For this chapter I want you to take a photo of yourself at this place in your journey. You can paste it here in your journal area or just frame it until the end of this book. I'll have you take another picture then too. Maybe you'll want to take a picture of your closet too. There will be many changes in there over a period of weeks and months. As you view it, take note of how you see changes in your chapter journaling pages in upcoming chapters. Take some time to pray for God to show you a glimpse of your true self.

Journal page for chapter three,
Opening Closet Doors

On these journal pages, I'd like you to focus on your worth, you are exquisite.

God has more *for you*. Open the door to the desires of your heart that are deep inside your mind. Open a new door, but get ready to embrace everything that it may bring. What part of you have you been hiding behind closed doors? What dreams were crushed by your events of abuse?

Cashmere Sweaters

Trust is something earned, sacred, safe and comforting. I like to think of trust as a warm soft cashmere sweater. Wearing it makes me feel safe, warm and cozy. When I first put it on, it is wonderfully comforting. I love to wear a cashmere sweater, watch movies and drink hot chocolate on a cold blustery day. Putting it on when I feel ill or emotional, it has the potential to change my mood to being comforted. We all have comfy clothes in our closets. They may not be cashmere but they are worn for the same reasons. We choose to find comfort in something or someone. Trust is something we give someone or something.

Trust is *so very precious* to me. I don't readily give it to anyone who hasn't earned it. It may take years for me to give it to someone and I may remove it as quickly as an instant if I feel threatened. I have a few longtime friends who have not only earned my trust, they continue to keep it. They are tried and true friends who have shown that their heart is towards me and want only for my best interests, even when they feel they need to tell me something painful or hard to hear. They know I need to hear what God is showing them for me to continue my growth in Christ. One close friend keeps asking me, when I ask her for advice, "Do you really want to know what I think?" I always say yes, because I know I can trust her to tell the truth and do it in such a way as to be so acceptable that I have to admit it and immediately I know that I need to change. Don't get me wrong, it still takes time for me to make certain changes in my life.

I chose them because they first of all love and serve the Lord Jesus themselves and second of all, they are honest, caring individuals who listen and will follow through for what is right, regardless of my mere fleshly feelings. Oh they let me have the feelings briefly but they don't let me get away with staying in my pity parties. It is hard to stay there when you know the truth of God's word and His love for you directly and through the kindness of others. They use God's word to assist and keep me accountable.

When I hear others talk about how some people are so controlling, I cringe because I have learned from experience that **controlling is a secondary issue**. It follows the real problem of a *lack or absence of trust in someone or something*. I find it almost difficult to submit to anyone whom I cannot trust. Who in their right mind would let go of their own control to someone who has harmed them or been unfaithful or unkind or untrustworthy in other areas of their lives?

Think about it. If you **did trust** someone it would be *easy* to let go of control. I know because—**as I trust—I relinquish control—almost instantly**. It just happens without my ever thinking about it. No decisions made, just reacting to being able to trust fully and inexplicitly.

For me, one of my life's journeys has been trusting God. Yes, it is true, trusting God has been, for me, a *journey*. I liken it to an adopted child. Leery of the one who adopted them.

Do they really love me? I'm not their real kid. I'm not anything special, no hidden talents, nothing to show for myself worthy of adoption let alone love of a stranger. What if I make mistakes, what if I don't measure up to their expectations? Will I really be loved? Will I be understood and believed in? Will anyone guide me and help me find my purpose? We are adopted by God into His Family. It is a glorious family. The holy realm family. I like the idea of Michael the Arch Angel, protector, being my big brother. Just try to mess with me, he'll be there. (That's not scriptural, just a metaphor.) Seriously, when we accept Jesus Christ as our Lord and Savior, we are wholly adopted to a holy family. They stick together and assist you in all life's challenges and trials. There is never a moment where that family doesn't give you all you need to complete a task or follow through with God's perfect designed plan for your life.

God as my father was a stretch for me. My dad died at age 30 and I didn't really know him much. So most of my life was without a father figure. I could only imagine what a father was supposed to be like. What I didn't know was **God wanted to be my father**. I learned that through hard times and hard lessons without trusting in HIM, trying to do it all myself. Looking like I was controlling, I really didn't know how to trust someone I could see, let alone one I couldn't see. Actually, writing this book has given me the insight, through Jesus Christ and the Holy Spirit, into this chapter on trust. I knew there needed to be a chapter on trust in the book. As I have prayed for wisdom for each chapter, He guides me and teaches me in the lessons before I can actually get anything on paper. I also am learning the lessons.

When you see anyone who seems to need to control others, or many aspects of their lives, you need to first look into what is behind that issue, to see what all is there. It is never as easy of an answer as you would think. Give them a chance to see it for themselves first, and then admit to you that there is a problem before judging them harshly. It isn't easy to find healing from past or current pain if we are always judged by everyone for our instant emotions or actions instead of our whole life's character.

Many of us have heard that those who control are doing so to make sure they don't get hurt, that is true to a certain point. We *feel* we cannot trust others with ourselves, our lives, or the decisions that have to do with ourselves, our children's lives. We sometimes feel we know what's best and pursue our thoughts or desires towards that goal for others in our lives as well as ourselves. When we feel others have let us down, we grip harder to being more committed to doing it all ourselves.

For us mothers, it is expected that we have control over our children. Anyone on an airplane hopes the mother has control over their child. However, with older adult children we need to pull back and let them learn through life lessons, which is best. They have to live out their choices and decisions as they get older. Controlling adult children or other adults is harmful because we cross the line of the other person's rights and their personal opinions and choices too. You have to relinquish control either voluntarily or involuntarily with your kids as they get older. If you fail to let go, they'll respond to your hovering as control and not want to include you on things, or they'll feel judged and think they'll never measuring up to your standards

You can let go of your adult children if you *trust in the Father God* to finish their upbringing. Let God put His knowledge in them to fulfill His perfect design, guided by the Holy Spirit to direct and protect their life. You can trust God for all things because He has a reputation, a proven record, a factual presence, innumerous accounts of promises upheld and fulfilled by any and everyone who will trust God for anything, large or small. All you have to do is begin.

What can you trust God for today? Make a decision now to start with any small or large thing and give it fully into the trust of God, *your Father, and Master Designer*. Watch and see what He has in store for you. Look for His perfection in His design for you and your life. He has your back, you can trust in Him explicitly, not just partly, but wholly, nothing hidden, nothing held back. He will prove to you His **power**, His **love**,

His **protection**, His **provision**, His **plan**, His **purpose** for your life and His **wisdom** in all things concerning you. You see all of creation and all that He has planned for the animals and their habitats and the food chain and all there is to the weather patterns and the amazing stars, rotations of the sun and moon, and He has a place for you, a unique purpose that only you can fill if you trust in HIM alone.

His plan needs no back up. His will *is His plan*. Led by the Holy Spirit, we will be able to finish what we were meant to become.

Fear and trust are good motivators. But fear also keeps us from trusting in the right things in our lives. We all start out as infants trusting until that trust was broken by some harmful or bad situation in our lives. Depending on the circumstance, we soon begin to develop our coping mechanisms to be able to handle the pain, and all that goes with the loss of part of our selves. I found out I have a few coping mechanisms. One being that I avoid persons that look like my abuser. Unfortunately there are a lot of great people who do look like that. I have had to modify my fear or avoidance by telling myself not all those whose appearance like that are abusers. Sight triggers our memories emotions. When I go into places similar to where I was abused, I get emotional about being in there and again I have to remind myself that there are many other reasons to be in that type of establishment. I have to walk that out too and make better memories in those places as well as let go of those old memories. This is part of PTSD, post-traumatic stress disorder, and finding a counselor could help you in your healing process here.

I love to dress up. However, one of my triggers is being stared at for all the wrong reasons and possibly targeted by perverted individuals. So I have two issues there, is my dress appropriate, if yes, then I have to ignore those who are sinful. If my dress is in any way inappropriate, then I need to change as to not draw all the wrong type of attention to myself. Let's face it girls, we do want some form of attention, but let that not be from our wrong type of clothing. Dress to impress, but make a good impression. Women who act and dress like ladies get the gentlemen. Make them step up to you. You don't need to dress down and overtly sexy to get a guy.

Some women purposefully wear clothing so baggy that no one would suspect they are female. Hiding themselves, thinking they are protecting themselves from further pain, rejection or abuse. Choosing to wear unflattering clothes everywhere we go can keep us from moving forward into new areas of growth in our lives. Don't hide yourself, instead find your own unique style and be comfortable in your own body shape that God gave you as a woman. Fashion is not form fitting for style; it is style that fits you and your lovely personality. Find new types of clothes and try them on to see what you may be missing. You may just shine brighter as the wonderful confident spectacular woman you really are.

I get so uncomfortable with compliments. My past is one of being deceived, so I question everything and want to know all the whys about a compliment. I have to learn to accept a compliment for what is said and be gracious and thank them politely and not question everything. I need to trust that it is sincere and to learn grace in it all.

We all *want* to trust in something, someone. We all want others to know we can be trusted in. It is the actions of ourselves and others that actually determines the level of trust we will have with one another. Trust can also be unsafe, harmful and disruptive to our souls if we put our trust in something or someone who is untrustworthy. If you have purchased a fake cashmere sweater it will not have the same effect as the real one. Say it is mixed with wool. We all know wool is warm, but it is not by any means soft, it is scratchy and some of us will have an allergic reaction to it and develop an itchy rash.

When it comes to trust we must take time to invest in the best quality. Search it out, who have you put trust in? I put my trust in God who is always there for me. Like you I have made decisions of misguided trust in other people. When that happens I have to make some decisions about the relationships.

When trust is broken we have several options to take.

- Continue in the relationship, working out the issues that broke trust, which takes both willing parties to accomplish, which may take time and counseling to overcome.
- Become an angry, agitated person who sees only one side of the issues, thus pushing the other one away with unforgiveness and bitterness.
- Complying with the other person to the point where you lose yourself respect and personhood in order to not confront the issues with an angry/hostile person.
- Pray over the situation first and finding the right counselor to help you decide if the relationship is worth fixing, or you may need to let that relationship go.
- Leave the relationship and all normal relationships and go into depression losing yourself all together and living life introverted and lonely.

Obviously there are many things we could do afterwards, but we need to consider that all choices have consequences. We have to choose the one that we can live with the rest of our lives. I want you to keep in mind that God is a God of reconciliation. His first design for all of us is to get along with each other. When that doesn't work, we should consider seeking a mediator to assist us with resolving the situation. Remember also, trust and forgiveness are two separate issues. Forgiveness is a requirement for our own salvation. He forgives us first, and then requires us to forgive others to keep our forgiveness, it is not an option. Although trust is not required to forgive someone, we must **en-trust** God with the situation. Casting all your cares upon Him for He cares for YOU! Don't miss the meaning behind that. Also, when we care for others we show a small amount of how much HE cares for each and every one of us.

Trust is freeing and wholly peaceful. You won't have full peace until you trust and relinquish your fears and hold on things you can't control anyway. Letting go doesn't mean you don't care, it means you are putting it fully upon the only One, who can do all things in perfect timing to completion and wholeness. Won't you let go and give Him your whole life, not just a small part. The Bible says we are His bride, He is our groom. He wants His bride to trust in Him fully. So what kind of relationship will you have with your heavenly Father? Your spiritual spouse Jesus? Will your story be a Cinderella story? I hope and pray you choose Jesus as your Prince Charming.

Journal page for chapter four,
Cashmere Sweaters

On this journal page I want you to focus on where you have, in the past, put your trust. What or who has violated your trust? What will it take for you to trust again? Pray for God to help you trust Him more in your life and destiny.

Corsets

Unforgiveness is like a corset that is too tight. They bind us and keep us from breathing easily, preventing us from freely moving. A corset will keep us from being all that we were meant to do and become. It is uncomfortable, causing us to become irritable. Sometimes we can be short and unnecessarily angry with others.

Forgiveness releases you from the bondage of your past.

Forgiveness is **not** just for the perpetrators, but for our own benefit. There is no other way to really let go of the pain and stop the negative feelings that go along with the remembrance of the abuse. Forgiving does not release the person who has harmed us from God's judgment. God is in control of that. He promises to be our Redeemer, our just judge.

I had to learn forgiveness after some unfortunate incidents. God told me I had to pray for the people who were involved in harming my family. I responded, "You have got to be kidding me! Are you for real or what? Can't you find someone else to pray for them? I do not want to do it. Really, are you serious? I don't want anything to do with them ever again. I want them out my family's lives. No way, I'm not going to do it!!" Well, let me tell you, the Holy Spirit kept telling me the same thing. "*Pray for them.* You want to take back what was once yours, great, do more and take back what is MINE. Take back from the devil that which are the spoils of war. Those that are unlovable to you are not unlovable to ME." Though still in my righteous anger, I prayed for their salvation and repentance of the evil they were doing to others. I told God, "Okay, but I'm only doing this because you asked me to." I prayed and prayed and slowly the anger in my heart and soul began to diminish. Not the pain right away, but the anger.

The Holy Spirit told me I had a spirit of murder in my heart and I knew he was right. I wanted justice for once in my lifetime. Every abuser that hurt me got away with it. I was more than furious! I was so protective of my daughters while they were young. No one can better understand what I went through than someone who has already been through it. I had to question my own faith in a God who would allow such a thing to happen. I had to rebuild my own faith that I thought was unshakeable. I had to confess that there is NO other God, than Jehovah. I had to go through a very long and painful recovery from those incidents. I know it is man's sinfulness and disobedience, which causes pain, not God. **It is never in God's will or plan for us to suffer.**

That's when I knew I needed help, so I contacted the Christine Ann Center, a shelter for abused women. I went to meetings where they discussed what abuse is and how to address it. The women came and supported each other in their time of distress. They listened to me and were encouraging, they never belittled me, nor shamed anyone. The group I was in was not a faith-based shelter, but I knew enough about God to take my healing from there, rebuilding faith, removing hate, learning to let go and let God be the judge to handle the abusers judgments.

Jesus said in Matthew 6:14, 15
"If you forgive men their trespasses,
your heavenly Father will also forgive you:
But if you do not forgive men their trespasses,
neither will your Father forgive your trespasses."

So I had a choice, we always have a choice, to forgive and be forgiven or vice versa. God is not a respecter of persons or sins. All sin is evil in God's eyes. There are no little white lies, or little sins, only SIN.

It is easier to let go of past painful experiences than constant ongoing ones. We begin to trust again and it is all stripped away when abuse occurs again in our lives. We face our nagging inner selves about our worth again and again, only to come up short. We will never answer the proverbial "whys" until we face our closets, inner and outer ones. Emptying them of all our old, unwanted, shameful, ill fit, ruined, unnecessary and ragged clothes of our past. They will only continue to bring the same ill feelings that keep us in the shame and emotional turmoil. ***So let's stop putting them on.***

Job 36:15
"He delivers the poor in his affliction,
and opens their ears in oppression."

First, we need to take the garment of unforgiveness, the corset, off. We have to take it off with God's help. Are you ready? There will never be a better time than now. Be strong and confident. This is the beginning of a new YOU. Carrying around the abusers remembrance is like having a dead part on your body. It begins to decay and create contamination on other parts of healthy flesh. If not treated soon, you will have gangrene and need to have limbs and parts cut off of you. It is not worth hanging on to it.

Pray for the abuser, for your loss and your pain. Cry, go ahead and keep crying until you have peace from God. It is a process. Let the Holy Spirit comfort you as you ask God to fill the empty painful places. Give God time to do that also. This is not a time to rush any of these important steps. You will need to ***keep praying through*** the times you are reminded of the past or abuser. Don't let satan deceive you into taking back your forgiveness. ***Do give it back to God, each and every time you do remember.*** You have had this in your life for a while, so it may take a while to shed it off your life. New things are hard for me too. That is why I know it will take time and obedience to God's word of forgiveness. Thank God for all he has brought you through and from. He has and will continue to be with you, even though we do not understand the "whys."

27

Secondly, forgiveness needs to be an everyday event. The person who cut us off in traffic. A rude person at the checkout. A friend who never calls us. When we get shortchanged by someone or left out of an event, we all feel hurt. It happens to us nearly every day. And let's not forget what is commonly known as "church hurt." That's when someone in the church family has knowingly, or un-*knowingly*, hurt us. We wrongly expect those who are called believers, Christians, to be completely pure and mature. We all have hurt someone at some time in our lives, no matter if we know or remember it. If we would want others to forgive us, then we need to forgive them as well. Some people are in so much pain they don't see what they do to others. Some incidents are so small but we can make them appear so huge. If we don't forgive them soon we will destroy relationships. So let's not let that happen. Pray and seek godly direction before you choose to talk to them. He can open up their hearts and minds to see what is going on better than anything we can say or do.

Scripture says in Matthew 18:15-17
"Moreover, if your brother sins against you, go and tell him his fault
Between you and him alone. If he hears you, you have gained your brother.
But if he will not hear you, take with you one or more witnesses, that 'by the
mouth of two or three every word will be established'. And if he refuses to
hear them, tell it to the church. But if he refuses even to hear the church, let
him be as a heathen and a tax collector."

Remember, not everyone will deal with those things like we would like them to. We need to extend grace to others just as we would want others to extend to us.

Always strive for restoration first. **Our God is the King of Restoration.**

In my opinion, moving mountains is easier than changing people's hearts, but He is more than capable to do so. I know, I have seen Him do it many times. Including moving **my heart**, when I was unmovable. Praying for those who have hurt us is so important. *Many a friendship has been saved and strengthened by honesty and forgiveness.* Who hasn't had a bad day or an emotional upheaval and said things we regret to others. Never, never, I repeat, **never assume anything**.

Thirdly, I have learned there are relationships that you just should not continue in. They become toxic and you are always left with a negative feeling after spending time with them. So, go ahead and politely discontinue those. No one should stay in a relationship that is unhealthy. Now I'm not saying if that relationship is a marriage to just dump it. No, that is another matter. Counseling and much prayer for the marriage relationship are good places to start. If however, this is an abusive situation, do separate yourself at least temporarily from harm and seek godly counsel. It is my opinion that you should not return until the abuser has had counseling as well.

You do not need the burden of harmful people in your life anymore. The remembrance of them and the abuse is a burden you can ask God to release you from. A burden is like a backpack. It is not a fashionable piece of clothing anyway. When did you last see a royal princess carrying a backpack? They have others carrying their things. Let God carry your past baggage. He will deal with it all and continue to help you heal as you grow in grace and knowledge of Him and His love for you. It will happen. I know the more I let him carry for me the less I have to carry. That goes for the people I worry about too. Letting go frees you and me to walk towards our destiny.

A destiny needs quiet focus.

A destiny also needs nourishment and healing that you will only find in Christ, with the Holy Spirit's teaching, leading and counseling.

Let the healing begin as you become lighter in spirit and heart after letting go. Do not be mistaken, God is big enough to handle all we give Him and more. Maybe this is a good time to put this book down, give Him some of your pain, and take the time to heal. Go ahead; I will be here waiting for you. No rush. You are of great value and you are worth taking the time for healing.

See you soon, but come back, I have great things, for you, to come.

DISCLAIMER:
   *If you are married, I am not saying you should let go of your marriage. Contact **www.focusonthefamily.com**

They offer assistance for anyone in need, and as always pray and ask the Father God to show you what to do next. How do you know if your husband may be saved through your witness of God's salvation to you also? If it is abusive in nature, or you are in any danger at all, you need to get OUT. Always protect your life first, then get counseling after. Try to reconcile the issues of the marriage before making any decisions to give up and divorce. Many situations take months and years to work through. Be patient. It may not be the fairy tale dream we were looking for, but it will be real life, real love. Peace and joy can be found in our relationships.

Closet purging time for, Corsets

Time to go into your physical closet. I specifically want you to pull out *any garment that reminds you* of any form of abuse. Anything that reminds you of the old, painful past abuse needs to go out. You can't afford to keep on reminding yourself by having it and seeing it. You may feel it can't be replaced, but you can't begin new if you keep the old baggage. As you do, pray for continued strength for your journey of healing. You want to replace those things that create a visual reminder, not keep them. What you do with them is up to you. Burn them, rip them go ahead get your anger out. Or you can choose to put them in Goodwill. You can even journal what it was and what you did with it, or how it made you feel getting rid of it.

You deserve to wear things that reflect the new you, the fabulous woman that you are.

Journal page for chapter five, Corsets

The journey will be a painful process and there are a lot of steps along the way. Take some time off from the everyday demands, consider taking a mini-vacation.

Forgiveness isn't always what it seems. First, there is the acknowledgement of the abuse. The pain gets worse thinking about it. Then just after feeling like a Band-Aid just got ripped off your wounds, I'm asking you to pour the ointment of forgiveness on them. Actually the ointment of forgiveness is poured out on you first from God. Write out your forgiveness to those you no longer can communicate with, or as practice pages for those still alive. Maybe you'll start out with how they hurt you, include your anger on paper. Or maybe just make a list of those you need to forgive. Reread them and pray over them before you send them out, if that is the right thing to do.

Shoes

Anyone who knows me long enough knows I adore shoes. I found out that in my father's family heritage, someone made and repaired shoes. Maybe I got my love of shoes from them. I vividly remember as a small girl, just before Easter, my parents would get each of us girls a brand new pair of white shoes. I loved it. I felt so very special in my new white Easter shoes.

After my father died, we couldn't afford a lot of new things. My grandmother, who worked at a thrift store, would have us come over to her house. We would take our shoes off and step on a piece of paper and she'd trace around our feet to get our shoe size. It usually tickled and we'd laugh. At birthdays, or Christmas, my grandmother would give us each a bag of clothes, a pair of shoes and a special trinket or toy. As a teen I wasn't as preoccupied with shoes as I am today. I love fashion now, and well, you just have to have the right pair of shoes!

One day stands out even more than the new Easter shoes. It was Christmas 2010. My husband and I were at Macy's. We aren't rich by any standards and I can rarely afford Macy's. Since I am always drawn to the shoe section, I meandered that way and my husband probably thought "Oh no, here we go again." He humored me anyway. I scoured the store for my size and *there **THEY** were*. Oh yeah, it was like Oooohhhhh myyyyyyy gooodnnnnesssss!!! I just have to have those shoes. Normally I don't get so greedy, but they were just the sweetest little things I could possibly imagine. A high heel, peep toe, champagne fabric and black lace over that with a black patent leather bow!!!!! As I cautiously walked over, okay maybe I ran, in my mind thinking I'd better get over there before someone scarfs them up. And maybe I was a bit cautious thinking it probably won't fit me since I can hardly find department store shoes to fit. But let me tell you when I picked them up and secretly drooled over them, I noticed they were size 6. Oh Bummer. That's okay, I'll just try them on for fun. To my utter surprise and total overwhelming emotion, they fit. Ohhhhhhhhh baby, come to mama!!! Deliciously, I stepped into both of them and walked a little bit and I was smitten. It was as if the angels were singing in chorus over me. Yeah, I felt like Princess Diana. No, I felt like Queen Elizabeth!! I reveled and let the sweet feeling of glorious joy and hope surrounded me. Then I looked at the price, it was over my budget. My heart was only slightly jilted since I kept saying "Oh I really love these. I really love these."

I tried to figure out how I could pay for them. I was trying hard not to use credit cards so that wasn't an option. As I was taking them off I noticed a green sticker on the box, my heart jumped for joy—a sale!! Could it be that these most wonderful shoes could actually be mine? I mean, MINE. I peered again and sure enough they were on sale. I asked the shoe clerk what the sale was and she said half off. Then she asked me a glorious question, "Can I wrap those up for you?" I wanted to scream yes and hurry, but I said, without hesitation and with much pride and secret delight, "Yes, please." I was so giddy and excited. They fit like heaven made them just for me and planted them there for my special gift.

I don't know if you are as shoe crazy as I am. You get the mental picture of how much a pair of shoes can make some of us feel, let alone make an outfit look spectacular! I am using my shoe fetish to make a point. What we wear on our feet does make a difference. How we dress our feet spiritually has a purpose as well. In scripture, Ephesians 6:15, it says, "Having shod your feet with the preparation of the Gospel of Peace." Shod, oh heavens, what does that mean? In the Hebrew dictionary it says that shod means, *"to start on a journey, move or go forward, be on your way."* This journey of peace is not only for our own healing, but also for sharing our healing with others. We know firsthand how there is no peace until a conflict has been resolved whether it's between countries or neighbors or families. We have an enemy. He knows you. He was thrown from Heaven and is jealous of anyone who chooses God over him. As if he really had anything to offer in the first place. He is only a duplicator and a very poor one at that. He is what fashion calls a cheap imitation, he only offers what we would call "knock offs." His quality is bad and his ads lie. In other words, I wouldn't buy a pair of shoes from him, or anything else for that matter.

What kind of shoes do we get outfitted with for our journey? There are several ways to look at that question. Our shoes are to be as the warrior's, against our enemy,★ but towards our fellow man, we need to wear shoes of peace. Shoes that welcome others into our churches, homes, hearts, towards salvation and peace for their souls. We don't want to trample the feet of our friends and neighbors. Stepping on toes is not a good way to establish peace. We all face temptations, but we need to fight against the enemy satan, and be at peace as much as it is possible with all people.

It is not *being right* that matters but in *doing* right that changes lives. So on your journey of healing you will be presented many opportunities to share what God has done for your life. You won't be perfect and that is okay. Use what you have learned and know to be true. That doesn't mean you are not capable of sinning, it just means *you have everything within you from God not* to fall into *temptation to sin.*

Jesus came and lived a sinless life and has shown us how we can conquer sin. With God's help, and the armor of God, we can overcome any temptation.★★ Any temptation! I am proof of that in my own life. The journey is a great one. It will have pitfalls. If we join forces, support each other on our journey, with encouragement, faithful and fervent prayer for each other, we will all make it to the other side. Won't you put on your shoes of peace and offer the same to a tired and needy soul? I am reaching out to you and if you reach out to others, we can spread the peace of a new life with Christ and how he has transformed us. Come, let's be on our journey and move on to greater heights, higher callings and greater victories!!! Together we can change the world with His gospel of inner peace. There is strength in numbers.

★ See appendix for more information on the New Testament's soldier's footwear.
★★ The Armor of God is found in Ephesians Chapter 6.

Closet purging time for, Shoes

For this chapter I want you to consider the type of shoes you would need for peace. Normally I would ask you to purge or remove something from your closet, but I want you to consider adding to it this time. Do you have in your closet any shoes that are for walking? Not just for exercise, I mean for getting out there and meeting people and ministering to their needs. Stilettos are great fun, but if you don't have any shoes for working with others, you are missing out on a lot of life. We all need each other. So if you don't own a pair of walking shoes, buy some. While you're at it, purchase a second pair that you can get dirty just in case. You can be in prayer about each day and who God will put in your path!

Journal page for chapter six, Shoes

Will you start your journey with peace? Peace in your heart, mind and soul? Journal here the ways you have wished for peace and haven't found any. Where is your path currently taking you? Will you arrive in Heaven using the path you're following now? Where will you get your peace from? What ways can you bring peace to your family, friends and the world?

Ruffles and Lace
(Grace)

Grace is a garment that is considered vintage these days. It used to be a standard female essence that cloaked the most well groomed woman. Queens and princesses and the wealthiest of women seemed to personify gracefulness. They were so ladylike and calm and serene, walking as if they did not have a care in the world. We all want to be beautiful, but to most of us graceful seems overwhelmingly girly and can be awkward for those who had more physical jobs and hobbies. Seems that today's worldly vision of graceful women, is that they are weak. I disagree. I believe that gentleness and meekness is strength under control.

A queen is trained to be graceful in manners and in decisions affecting her kingdom. She can't run off willy-nilly on her emotions and still carry on with her royal duties as the queen. She has a position that reflects her upbringing, her royal heritage and her people. How well she reacts to situations that come across her path every day proves how she rules the kingdom. She doesn't get a break. It is her **life's purpose**. Her life is for her country, not merely for her own selfish needs or wants.

You can train someone to be physically graceful. It becomes a woman to be graceful. A man will change his actions to meet the standards of the female he is pursuing. Upgrade your value inwardly. Choose those whom you are around very carefully, keeping **your best future** in mind. You will see the difference not only in yourself and your dreams being fulfilled, but also in who is attracted **to you**.

Although grace is an outward garment that others see in us by our actions and behavior towards others, like a queen, it is actually something that becomes a part of us when we **accept** grace. I really don't think there is much difference between graceful and grace-full. Being full of the grace of God, embodying our hearts minds and souls, we then automatically live out what we have inside of us. With God we can become graceful, calm, serene, knowing full well we have all we need, walking like we own a part of the world, because we do. Our heavenly father owns all of it and we are His princesses. Walk in your glorious womanhood, which God graciously gave you. **It isn't a place of shame, but of honor to be a woman.** Just like the queen, we have a position to fulfill.

It may take a while before you feel full of grace but it will personify you as well as the most elegant graceful woman you can think of. Casting your cares on Him for He cares for YOU. That is how you can walk around without a care in the World. Your heart will be set on Heaven and your worries will all be taken care of.

The Bible's definition of grace is unmerited favor. That means you can't earn it. You can't buy it, nor steal it, nor borrow it. Favor, when is the last time you heard that? Have you been shown favor in the workplace? Maybe you earned it by your own hard work. Have you seen it in family relationships? Maybe you were the one spoiled or you were the one left out. Either way we all have a chance to have GRACE. You have the same opportunity as anyone else to receive it and be blessed by the gift of it. I do not know any girl who wouldn't *love* a gift from someone they knew loved them. A gift with no strings attached. How absolutely lovely!

Grace is a garment we choose to wear. It is a gift from the Father God. Envision this with me:

> You are presented with a beautiful 4 foot by 2 foot by 10 inch large box, wrapped in glistening white paper and a huge satiny red bow. The red bow signifies *the sacrificial blood of the Lord Jesus Christ for redeeming our lives back to the Creator God*. The beautiful glistening white wrapping paper is called *forgiveness*. The card on the box is *your invitation to Salvation and an inheritance with the King himself*. He also promises to adopt you and take care of you for the rest of this earthly life *and* the next one *in* Heaven *with him*. The gift in the box is a *white garment of exquisite fabric only made in Heaven*. It is fashioned for your character and fitted for you with your unique measurements. The Designer had your life specifically in mind, and with nothing else but *love in His heart for you*. He prepared this gift and many more for You.

Would you like to know what happens if you *do* accept the package and open it? It is so wonderfully amazing! Startling and so refreshing! Better than the air after the rain so fresh, and free. Better than peace after a war. It brings a wholeness to your very core, your entire soul and body and mind and spirit. The forgiveness alone empties your greatest fears and torments and shame. New experiences of hope arise, as you trust in the plan that He designed just for you. Remember, He is Your Master Designer. He is your personal Designer.

He knows all your intricacies and flaws and how to "dress" those to make you look, feel and become great! He knows what it will take for you to shine. We give up on our dreams because we think we have to do all of it ourselves. We forget that He has made us for a specific purpose and He intends for us to fulfill it and He will give us *whatever* it takes to complete our "mission". He never wants us to fail. We only fail when we leave out the Designer. "I know the plans I have for you, plans for a future and a hope," says the Lord.

I love to sew, but I hate to rip out seams. Can I do it? Yes, but I'd much rather design than tear apart a dress. It takes way longer and more mental work and sometimes it is irreparable. But God isn't like that. He loves a good challenge. We can all be a challenge after we have gone our own way, or made some bad choices in life. He will not ever give up on us. John 3:16 states, "Whosoever," that means anyone, "confesses their sin and repents"—that means turn around and not go back to the sin, "and choose to believe on the Lord Jesus shall be saved."

Grace, will you be wearing it or leaving it in your closet? It won't go away even if you choose to ignore it at this time of your life. It will always be there just waiting for you to open it and begin a new part of your journey. This garment is the most comfortable one you will ever wear. There isn't anything like it in this earthy world. You will never feel the same about yourself ever again.

New garments are exciting to buy and wear, but this one is offered to you for free. His offer to you is precious and you are worthy of the gift, because you are wonderfully and beautifully made—precious in His sight are His children. Want to be one of them? I do! Oh, I am. Come join me and be my sister on this journey of life. I love chick flicks and sisters make the best of friends. Won't you be one of mine?

Closet purging time for,
Ruffles and Lace

For this chapter I want you to consider having a tea party. It can include any venue of food or drink but make it a special event by inviting your closest friends and have them dress up. Often times we don't dress up for any occasion, but this is different. I want you to experience a Tamar "princess" moment. Enjoy the gracefulness of etiquette and fine dining. Or maybe you prefer to get all dolled and go out to eat at a restaurant, with either friends or a mate. Either way enjoy the time, you deserve it. Maybe you'll venture out of the box and get a tiara too! Princess practice!

Journal page for chapter seven,
Ruffles and Lace

I know I may have a different sense of what a woman is than you might have, but I hope you will indulge me for the sake of this book. Write on this page what you thought of the gift box delivered to your door? The gift of a white raiment, a beautiful gown. Did you open your gift? What keeps you from accepting the gift? Can you accept grace from God? Are you willing to pass on grace to others?

Accessories

I love to use accessories. Accessories are what you add to a wardrobe. They are not the main garment, but they can add or distract to an existing outfit. Adding color, shape, style, bling, they can even change the appearance of poor sizing.

When I had gone to the Christine Ann abuse shelter for classes, I was asked if I wanted a scarf. At first I thought, "I don't really need this as much as someone else might." But then I realized, **someone thought about ME.** They made a scarf for someone who was in pain and possibly in fear, living in a woman's shelter for safety. I was in so much pain, but I always thought that someone else was worse off. I finally had to admit I needed help, love and support too. The person, or people, who made those scarves were thoughtful and giving of their resources and talents. Their small gesture of kindness touched my heart and still does. To me the scarf is an accessory of hope, the kindness of a stranger to me, a wounded woman.

Before you put on an accessory, you first have to plan your main garment.

Salvation and baptism give you white garments to wear. So what do you add to that? White goes with almost anything, but you don't want to make your new white garments appear trashy. You'll want to be careful to only *add to* the garment, not take away from its purity. Anything you add to your life is considered an accessory. There things you'll add that are also spiritual. They will accessorize quite nicely with your spiritual garments. Here are some essentials that I think are the best accessories for a woman who intends on changing her life and the world around her. You want others to see your accessories too, not just the garments. Your life will be full having added these to your spiritual "jewelry" box.

2 Peter 1: 5-8
"And beside this, (salvation) giving all diligence,
add to your faith—virtue; **add to virtue**—knowledge;
Add to knowledge—temperance; **add to temperance**—patience;
add to patience—godliness; **Add to godliness**—brotherly kindness;
add to brotherly kindness—charity.
For if these things be in you, and abound, *you shall* neither *be*
barren nor unfruitful in the knowledge of our Lord Jesus Christ."

We begin with our *faith in Christ.*
- Then add to that *virtue,* which means the quality of moral righteousness or excellence. It also includes sexual purity.

- Then add more *knowledge* in your life. We can do that through reading and studying the Bible and also expanding ones knowledge through furthering your education.
- *Temperance* refers to moderation; self-restraint in conduct, expression, indulgence of the appetites, etc., basically self-control in all areas of our lives.
- *Patience* is added because even though we think we have it initially we soon find that we run out of it quickly. Patience is the ability to wait without complaining. I certainly could do better with that one.
- *Godliness* refers to having a desire to serve God with all your heart, obeying His word and following the Life of Christ who embodied God.
- *Brotherly kindness* is simple enough. To care for each other as we would our own "brother," which also includes neighbors, family, friends, and acquaintances.
- *Charity* is the love of God for humanity. It also means giving financially to those in need. We should all give as we are able to those in need. You never know when you may be in need of someone else's charity.

Another accessory to consider is our friendships. Our life is enriched by having others in our lives. Take inventory of those relationships. Do they complement your life or take away from your best life. We will always have those who need us, but some people seem to drain all you have and never really want to change their lives for the better. If you are enabling them in any way, then change your approach to that relationship. If you are a new believer, you will want to make new friends that are also Christians. It will be easier not to be around those who try to keep you down or in illegal or immoral lifestyles. We do become like those we spend time with the most. Spend time getting to know people you admire and want to be like. Having your own destiny, you will not want to follow their exact life, but it is good to have them mentor you.

Proverbs 18:24a
"A man *that has* friends must show himself friendly."

Be the kind of friend that you would like someone else to be for you. We all need someone to help us along the way. Life can get pretty cloudy and difficult. A smile and a hug are good ways to accessorize your life, and who couldn't use a good word of encouragement. Compliments and polite words are good accessories to use at home as well as at businesses and restaurants. A waitress is not a servant to you, she serves you, just as Christ served his disciples. They didn't belittle him for his service. Do be kind and compassionate to everyone. We're all precious in His sight. When Moses came down from the mountain, his face shone and they knew he had been with God, because God's glory shone on him. Be so close to God that you shine with His glory too. Others will be drawn to you as a result of your Godly accessories and want to be around you too.

Keep your life and emotional state current and fresh, forgive daily, hourly if necessary. Don't let it become full of unhealthy emotions or thoughts. Remember, emotional backpacks are not for princesses, let God carry your burdens and woes.

Closet purging time for, Accessories

Go through your purses, luggage, and jewelry boxes and, if you are brave enough, your desk drawers. Eliminate everything you can that reminds you of any past painful experiences. Maybe you need to get rid of some pictures of past people. Remember, our accessories are to add to our lives, not take away. You will feel freer from the experience.

Journal page for chapter eight, Accessories

What godly attributes, or "jewelry," will you be wearing? What relationships do you need to remove from your life or make adjustments to? Pray for courage to do so and wisdom to know who and how to make those changes. Who will you add to your life that will be a positive force for you in your journey?

Belt of Truth

How many belts do you have in your closet? Which ones do you wear most often? Belts are made of fabric, leather, gold or silver toned, beaded or studded or just plain black. Belts are used for many purposes. We all use them for each our own reasons. Maybe we use them for holding up our pants or skirts. Some people may use them for decoration at the hips to accentuate a fashionable style. Others may use them to cinch their waists in order to give a more hourglass shape to a dress or shirt. The truth is like a belt representing many things in our wardrobe, and spiritual life as well.

When we wear a belt for the sake of holding up our garments, it is like a comfort to us, a reassurance that we don't have to worry about a garment malfunction in front of others. We feel undone if we don't constantly appear all together in public. If we feel inadequate we become unfocused, distracted by the possibility of being vulnerable to embarrassment and others scrutiny.

Keeping it all together is hard to do when we are in such a state of mind that some or all things seem disorderly in our lives. Get to know which areas of your life feel like they are falling down around you. Truth is painful only if you continue to keep the lies surrounding each area.

When there is disorder anywhere, we can overcome it. Our closets tend to be a place easily cluttered. Decisions begin with, what size we really are, to who are we kidding, we aren't kids anymore. Most likely our wardrobes no longer reflect our present lives, desires or likes anymore. Possibly, you will find decades of personal changes, both good and bad. Purchases from mood swings, changes from singleness to married, having children, from student to career. Not to mention fads and all the extreme things we try to feed our self-worth. Taking the time to inventory your closet during each chapter will help you further your progress emotionally too. Another reason for this book, to clean out our closets!

When I was preparing for this chapter, I began to think about my own life and the truths I needed to learn for myself. I had a lot of clothes that were very mundane. Boring to say the least. Some were soiled and paint stained. I had lived my life pretty much a homebody. Which meant I didn't go out much and didn't have many nice things. Oh I had a few formals for weddings, my three daughters all got married within three years. I had a few dresses for church and maybe a pair of dress pants.

When I went to work I had to begin building a professional set of clothes. I had to *refocus* on who I was and dress appropriately. I was now a business woman, so my purpose for the clothes I chose to wear was job related. The clothes in your closet probably reflect your position at work, whether or not you work outside the home, the type of hobbies you have, and whether or not you participate in sports.

The truth about your life is in your wardrobe. What are those clothes saying to you? Do they reflect where you want to go in life? Do they show you at your best or bring you down when you wear them? Do you need to purchase some other garments to get you to where you want to go in life?

One truth for me is that I look better in a dress due to my shape. I have tried to wear fashions that were the current fad, but my shape just couldn't pull it off. So I have learned the truth about myself that my shape has to come first for picking the style of what I wear. There are many books on that so I won't address it here, but your body shape is who God made you. I have to be thankful to God for mine, even though I am not tall or thin. I decided to watch and see what the celebrities are wearing that have my shape and wha-laaa, try it for myself. They all have flaws too, they just know how to cover them with fashion. I'm still getting used to being in my own skin. I am getting better though as I learn the truths about who I am. It is ok to like yourself for who you are, and move forward, enriching your life and growing into a new version of yourself that is successful too. When you find the truth of who you are in Christ, you will hopefully see value in yourself enough to wear clothes that reveal your value too.

Truth can be found in other areas of our lives. One in particular for me was in my home. I hate paper clutter, but somehow it seems like I always have several piles that I need to go through. They keep piling up and creating a mess, which then creates a need for more drawers for storage until I know what to do with them. Argh, it never ends.

One day I decided to focus on the real problem, hmmm what could it be? What is the truth here? Well, what I learned recently that I had a problem with making decisions. Those papers required me to make a decision, send money to someone, and write a letter, sales flyers, buy now or wait for later? Decisions, decisions, decisions! Yuck.

It was easy for me to throw it all out after it was outdated, but I had great difficulty making those decisions. I can make many decisions very quickly and others with careful deliberate calculated facts. However, this paper craze still has me baffled. So if I focus on only the truth in each of those papers it will bring me to a decision quicker.

- Truth: I don't have money, so I can't purchase sale items now.
- Truth: God will provide for my needs, and my wants, as I learn to trust Him.
- Truth: I cannot do all this financial stuff myself, I'm need some help on this.
- Truth: I don't have time to read all of these magazines. Someone else can enjoy them, and as I give them away and I can then enjoy a clutter free desk. Yay ME!
- Truth: those clothes don't really fit my body shape or flatter me, move them on.

I used *my truth* in this area of clutter and my piles are smaller now. I am learning I am not perfect at my decision process, but I will continue to start with truth, for each thing in my life that is out of order or cluttering my life. Sentimental items only have so much room too. I know of one woman who took pictures of her child's artwork and put them in a scrapbook for the child. We just can't keep everything! I feel so much better and together by making just that one simple adjustment of asking myself, "What is the truth here?"

We want others to see us as put together, nothing hanging out. When we add accessories, we feel the need to complete something, change something, or dress up our outfit. We try to draw attention from our flaws to better-proportioned parts of our selves, by using the accessory. You'll notice a belt of design before you notice the hips for instance. But first we need to know the truth and the truth will set you free. We all have faults and it is okay. That is why God sent Jesus to forgive us of our faults, our sins, bad decisions etc.

God says His word is truth. He knows the plans He has for you, plans for a future and hope. Plans for good and not evil and He means it. He has good things stored up for you. He has created a place for you in heaven. Yes and not any old shack either, a place in His kingdom where love rules, He is love.

Let's all make sure we don't draw attention to the flaws of others so we won't be noticed for our own faults. Whether it is about clothing styles or beauty or social standards, be an encouragement to all others. You don't know what happened in someone's upbringing or life's challenges. Take me, for instance. I am so uncomfortable with the idea of make-up. Being very intimidated as a teen, I only used Mascara. I am now at an age where I know what I want and am willing to make changes to get to my goal. I try hard to move forward and not let others dictate my value or standard of life.

Satan never tells the whole truth.

The enemy, satan, knows truth also. Remember, he was an angel before the Lord, day and night. Satan was so full of pride he decided he wanted to become as God. Satan knows enough truth about you that he uses it to first **bait** you, then **trap** you, then **torment** you, then push you up in front of God in **judgment** and say "Look what she did." For example: I wasn't treated fairly, nor appropriately by many people, so **satan's** twist on that truth was "You're not good enough to be treated right." which of course is a lie. The *whole truth* is that God is still who He says He is and has promised to take care of all that is His. God's truth is that HE loves us and we are worthy of love and kindness.

There were a few times I had thought of suicide. One time I actually felt like satan had entered the car and told me to drive into the river. The children were in the car and the *truth* was I would never ever harm them. That truth helped me to realize it was a lie from satan and I did not listen to the voice. Later, satan tried to get me to hurt myself by cutting my fingers off in a moment of inner pain. Since my mind thinks ahead so much *I knew the truth*; I was going to regret that decision. I didn't do that either. I see why people cut themselves, the inner hurt and pain seems to require some sort of release of physical pain, to have control over something. I *do not* however, support that, nor endorse such things. I am simply saying, "I get it, I know you are in pain, but don't do what the voices tell you. Focus on God and He will lift you up over this thing, if you trust Him." Be patient; do not be in a hurry to make your own changes. Seek Godly counsel and stay on your knees until you get relief from God, not the world's version of relief. The world has nothing of significance to offer you, it only compounds the problems, never alleviates them. I know, because there were times I wanted out. I was so lonely that satan kept sending me other lonely people to push me to sin.

Admittedly, I was tempted on several occasions, but I feared God and couldn't follow through. *I know the truth* in scripture says that even if you look to lust it is sin. I did sin, since it was in my heart to long for someone other than my spouse.

What holds you together? What truths will you uncover in your closet, both emotional and clothes closets? What truth will you choose for your guiding light in a tumultuous world? I am hoping and praying that you will experience God's truth in His word, His letters to you. Let truth free you from your past and your negative perceived images about yourself or others. I hope you will continue to join me on this journey of healing and seek truth for yourself and live the truth of your designed destiny that God has planned for you. It may seem hard right now but it will get easier. I promise.

Remember, I am also on this journey. I know you have pain. God knows it too and He is there for you all through your journey. It wasn't an accident that you are reading this book. I believe God puts people and events together for a reason.

Let's do this together and see what's next. Take your time through these chapters, they all have a purpose. Your life also has a wonderful purpose. Don't you want to find out why you were created? Keep on, my sister, we are getting close to our true selves.

Closet purging time for, Belt of Truth

For this chapter I'd like for you to open those closet doors wide and take a good look at everything in your closet. Do the clothes in there still represent who you really are? Do they tell the truth about your value? Is it possible your real self is lost in a sea of old clothing? Pray and ask God to help you see value in yourself as He sees you, not as the abuse from others has made you feel. You may want to get rid of those garments that don't fit your shape, your real value, or where you are heading.

How disorganized is it? Let the truth reveal itself in your decisions of what you keep and why. Sometimes it's easier to take it all out and see the sheer volume of items. Then separate them and see what organizational containers or shelves your closet needs. There are so many options for closet organization now. Almost every store has something for closet organization; baskets, bins, wooden shelves with drawers and elaborate shelving systems; shoe racks for hanging shoe holders and under the bed shoe containers, hangers have so many options too. If you need help with this project, go ahead and get help. I want to encourage you to get yourself as organized as possible. Not only will you know where everything is, you will feel good about opening the doors to your closet. You don't have to color coordinate it all, but enjoy the results. I am always surprised after I organize how much stuff I never use anymore and need to move it on so others can enjoy.

Journal pages for chapter nine, Belt of Truth

What truth about yourself did you learn as you looked over all your clothes? Did your closet fill up with clothing unsuitable for your value? Or have you begun to build a closet that reflects a strong woman who is going places? Journal those things down.

There are things in our lives that are also disorderly. Make a list of those things, or areas of your life, that you feel are out of control. Pray about each area and seek the truth in those areas first before you just go dive in and try and make the changes on your own. Don't rush this process of finding truth in it first. It will make the difference between temporary release of "clutter" and permanent healing inside and out. It is good to have a friend be your accountability for this project. They may know more about your truths than you think. I suggest daily making a list of priorities and practice sticking with them. You can also try putting them on a calendar or on your phone will help too. Setting deadlines for projects helps me too.

Dirty Laundry
(Shame)

Sometimes people in our lives use words that may seem like they are forcing us to feel dirty and to wear the garment of shame. Speaking blaming words, accusing us of wanting abuse, telling us we need them, telling us we do not account for anything apart from them, diminishing our worth. We've been told lies of all sorts. Maybe, worse yet, they were saying words of a threatening nature, promising harm to us or our loved ones. Possibly threatening us or exposing something about us, whether it is true or not. The wrong person wears the garment of shame. It was never meant to be worn by the victim of crime, whether abuse or any other violation.

2 Samuel 13:13a
"And I, [Tamar] where shall I cause my shame to go?
and as for you, [Amnon] you shall be as one of the fools in Israel."

Tamar experienced shame similar to what we might have. Very personal and private. Here in 2 Samuel she says, "***Where shall I go with my shame***?" Maybe she wondered, "I am a royal princess, who can I share my pain with? Who will keep it private? Who will understand my shame? Who will help me remove the shame?" Questions we all ask ourselves after an abuse has occurred. Unless you are in the media spotlight, you will not have to worry about paparazzi cameras or cheap magazines slandering your words and watching your every move. Tamar had a lot to worry about. Her shame had to stay a secret. How awful for her to have to bottle up all that emotional pain. I don't know if you are still hiding abuse from friends and/or family. It won't help your healing to keep the ones closest to you in the dark about what happened. They may be wondering what has changed in you, as no one can remain the same after being robbed of their own personal safety and violated. If it is too embarrassing, first try counseling specific to the type of abuse you went through. You may have to see a few different professionals before settling on one. I tried three and they are all different. Pray before you look for a counselor, ask others who have been through similar events who they have seen. My friend suggested the VA for my husband and myself because of our unique situation. That is where she found the greatest help for her, and since my situation was similar to hers, we decided to try it. You will know if they are the right one when you feel safe and the sessions get easier to handle.

In the dictionary, ***Shame*** is listed as: 1. a *painful* feeling of having lost the respect of others because of the improper behavior of oneself or (actions of) others. 2. Dishonor or disgrace (to bring disgrace to a family) 3. a *person that brings shame*, dishonor or disgrace. The dictionary also lists **Shamed** as; 1. to *cause to feel ashamed*, make ashamed. 2. to dishonor or disgrace (someone).

Looking at those definitions, we can distinguish from "***being shamed***" and "***causing shame***". We were shamed **by** someone. However, **we are not shame**. We **are not** shameful. Let's take that awful garment of shame off and figuratively put that garment of shame on the abuser, where it rightfully belongs.

Here are some scriptures that confirm **<u>who</u> the shameful one actually is**:

Psalms 35:26
"Let *them* <u>be ashamed</u> and brought to confusion together *that rejoice at my hurt*:
Let *them* <u>be clothed with shame</u> and dishonor *that magnify themselves against me*."

Psalms 132:18
"His enemies' will I (God) clothe with shame:
But, ***upon himself** (herself) **shall his** (her) **crown flourish**."*

God thinks about those who are harmed and promises good to those who seek after Him. I want to help you to walk a new emotional path. Leave the shame behind. Put off feeling responsible for the events around the shame. The above scripture says we will have a crown and we will flourish also. With our heads held high and our hearts renewed. Let's keep moving forward and owning our promises from God that we are marvelously made, and He loves us so much.

If you are married, and the abuse was from outside the home, this will definitely affect your relationship. I strongly suggest going together for 'couples counseling.' It will benefit your marriage to have a middle person involved during your time of healing. It will give the situation more clarity and the process will be more effective when you and your mate are on the same track. No one should minimize abuse. You should not minimize what happened to you and no one else should either. Those who do are just ignorant to the effects it has on the victims. On the other hand, you should not continue to play the victim role for the rest of your life either; nor spread malicious gossip about the persons involved. Hurting people hurt others and healed people heal others. Let's strive to become healers.

Counseling doesn't replace prayer for your own healing. I have prayed my way through a lot of awful days of remembering and hurtful times in my life. I have cried a sea of tears and felt so lonely, I actually felt physically cold. It took a lot of prayer and faithfulness to God that I was able to believe I am worthy of being His child. Not because I'm so great, but because I accept His offer of adoption through salvation.

I first recommend <u>Focus on the Family</u>. I have called them in the past and found them truly helpful and caring. I received help and prayer, direction and book advice also. They offer free services and resources. Focus on the Family also has a radio program on many stations as well, offering advice on several family issues. Check local programing or see the site online for where and when.

They can be contacted by internet at www.focusonthefamily.com, also look for "Focus on the Family Help Center,"

To speak with a family help specialist, call 1-800-A-FAMILY (232-6459) Monday through Friday between 6:00 a.m. and 8:00 p.m. Mountain time

You can also E-mail them at: help@FocusontheFamily.com

Look also for church listings, ask if they have help for women specific to your needs. They may also have local listings for other programs in your area. PTSD, post-traumatic stress disorder, counseling is not always easily found, but keep asking for it. They offer more extensive counseling for abuse than general counseling does.

Also check your local listings for Women's Shelters. They will offer options for safety, shelter and support as well as training.

Closet purging time for, Dirty Laundry

Shame is a garment that reminds us of our painful past; a garment to be tossed out of our lives and closets. Empty all your old, unwanted, shameful, ill fitted, ruined, and ragged clothes of your past from your closet. They will only continue to bring the same ill feelings that keep us in shame and emotional turmoil. ***So let's stop putting them on.*** Are there any clothes that makes you feel inadequate, shameful, make you feel bad about yourself or cause you to feel unworthy of greatness? Consider tossing anything that makes you feel less than your truth, you *are* worthy of greatness. We are on a journey of healing and self-awareness, self-worth and a move towards a great destiny. After all, we are the daughters of a KING. Ask yourself this one question: Would it fit in a princess' closet? If not, then why is it in yours?

Journal page for chapter ten,
Dirty Laundry

I hope you were able to understand that the garment of shame isn't yours to wear. I'd like for you to write down on this journal page, all the negative words spoken to you, all the shameful feelings you have had surrounding the abuse, and afterwards the feelings of being lost and the loneliness of your heart. Please include the stigma, or disgrace you have been through due to the abuse. I know this is hard but the healing gets easier when we open up. Remember these are lies about our real worth. The abuser wears the shame, not us. We are marvelously made for greatness!

Dancing Clothes
(Garment of Praise)

When I think of a garment that represents praise, I think of a white or maybe pink, light green, or yellow flowing dress. It might have ruffles or free floating sleeves. It is non-restrictive and allows freedom to dance and praise. It is to be a joyful garment to wear. Maybe it has flowers and ribbons on it. I do love to embellish.

Isaiah 61:3
"To appoint **unto them that mourn** in Zion, to **give unto them beauty for ashes**,
the **oil of joy for mourning**, the **garment of praise for the spirit of heaviness**."

The garment of praise *for* the spirit of heaviness. Sounds like a doctor's order—put on praise when you have a spirit of heaviness. Heaviness, does that sound familiar? I know I have felt heavy many times in my life, not only due to abusive situations but sometimes life just hits you hard. The above scripture also refers to mourning. Are you experiencing mourning? Maybe it's your dreams, improper relationships with others, lost virginity, lost childhood or not being treated right by others that you are mourning. Unlike the garment of grave clothes, mourning is different.

Mourning is a great sadness due to a great loss of something near and dear to us.

2 Samuel 13:19
"And Tamar put ashes on her head,
and ripped her garment of different colors that *was* on her,
and laid her hand on her head, and went on crying."

Tamar was in mourning over her abuse. She feels devastated and rips her princess gown. The King's virgin daughters all wore specific gowns that represented purity and virginity. She was no longer a virgin. She was in mourning. It was a great loss to her. It wasn't her pride, it was her right to be pure and remain a virgin till marriage. Her rights to a marriage at all were taken away from her, because of her culture and position at that time in history and purity can never to be replaced.

In the Bible they would cover themselves in ashes after great tragedies, whether it was personal, political or spiritual. Maybe you have felt like you wanted to cover yourself with ashes, feeling like you are only worthy of a heap of ashes. I have mourned what will never be. I've mourned not having a protector over me to keep the abuse from ever happening. I mourned what should have been a pure sexual relationship with my spouse. Past abuse sets you up for many problems. Fear of intimacy, fear of being mistreated or being taken advantage of. Nothing seems pure anymore after someone else has taken away your rights and introduced you to things you should not have ever known. You have to learn to trust and love again. First trusting God and then others.

After a period of mourning, the Israelites would anoint themselves with oil. The scriptures mention "the oil of joy." I'm not saying mourning turns into joy just like that. However, after our time of mourning, we need to start focusing on things that bring us joy.

The dictionary lists joy as, "a very glad feeling, happiness; great pleasure; delight." When I'm bummed for a long time, I do something fun to break up the boring monotony of life. One time I wore a clown nose to work on a Friday. Yes really, Haa haa. I worked in direct sales, calling small stores selling products. So, my customers never saw the clown nose, but my co-workers and supervisors did. We couldn't help but laugh and I kept it on for four hours. You may not do a clown nose but find some way to bring fun back into your life. I love a good romantic movie or chick flick when I feel down. Maybe it's a spa day for you or a manicure. Do something special just for you. We have a reason to rejoice.

Praise is listed as, "a simple word implying an expression of approval, esteem, or commendation." For example: Heroes are praised for their bravery. In our churches, we sing praise hymns to God. Laud is the word for extravagant great praise to God. Think about a time when you praised someone for a great deed that they have done for either yourself or someone else. What did you do to show them praise? To show them honor? How much more do you think God deserves our praise? He has done great things for you and will continue to do so because He loves you. Our Pastor always says to give God an "anytime praise." Give God praise even in bad times. He is still God in our bad days and He will bring us through everything in our lives. You may not always feel like God is there for you. I tell people, when you can't hear God, and don't know what to do or where to go, praise Him. Put on some praise and worship music and sing to Him. When I listen to praise music I feel so much better. I can put things in a better perspective when I honor God first and then let my worries go to God. The word of God says, "He inhabits the praises of His people." **He will meet you in your praise.**

Psalms 30:5

In His presence is fullness of Joy

That means when we seek Him we will find joy. We won't find joy in having things or eating our way into oblivion. That is only temporary happiness, or brief delight. We find it *in Him.* Are you ready to remove your mourning clothes? The garment of praise is light and free. After a hard winter in Wisconsin, we love to get back to our summer clothes. They are airy, free, fun and flirty. Are you tired of the heavy burdened garments of mourning? Try praise, you can do it anywhere and for as long as you like. Put on the garment of praise for the spirit of heaviness and be free.

Revelations 3:18
"I counsel thee to buy of me gold tried in the fire, that thou may be rich;
and *white raiment [garment of salvation]*, that thou may be clothed,
and *that the shame of thy nakedness do not appear*;
and anoint thine eyes with eye salve that thou may see."

When I read those scriptures they gave me goose bumps. God will put to shame our abusers. But more than that, He promises we have a white raiment and a crown to wear. And did you notice? It says, that if we wear the white raiment, *our shame will not appear*. It won't be there anymore. How is that possible? We can take shame off and put on the white garment of purity, salvation. And, if we follow in Christ's footsteps, we will be with Christ in heaven with God our Father when our time on earth is done.

Christ was abused and many sought to murder him. He was publicly beaten and was put to an open shame on the cross outside the city where only the loathsome sinners were left to die. But he chose to endure it so that we would know **He understands our sorrows and our pain**. However, His story didn't end on the cross. Oh no, it is an eternal story. He is seated at the right hand of The Father God.

I hope you can remove your garment of shame now and refuse to put it back on, regardless of who put it there. If someone continues to try to make you wear it, don't do it. Let the joy of a new white garment and crown be your focus. Remember you are, if you choose, a princess in God's royal family. No more sorrow, no more shame.

Come my sister, my friend and join me in praise to our Father God and His Son, Jesus. They are worthy of our praise. No one else can do for us what they have done. Rejoice my sister, be awakened by praise from your slumber of pain and sorrow. Live the life you were meant to live. Don't have any praise music? Look online for the nearest Christian book store, or just shop online for praise and worship music and listen to the samples. Pick the style you like and just become one with Him in praise. Sing it in the car, the shower, the exercise room, doing laundry. Doesn't matter where, just that you do it. When I was happy and joyful I used to put on praise music and when everyone was in bed, I'd play it and dance and sing to the Lord. It was fun and worshipful. Maybe one day you'll dance too!

Psalms 30:11
"You, O God, have turned my mourning into dancing;
You have put off my sackcloth and clothed me with gladness."

Closet purging time for, Dancing Clothes

Time to purge the old mourning clothes and put on praise clothes. Take a look in your closet and see what you own that has felt like death to you. Mourning clothes are usually black. If your closet has a lot of dark dreary clothes, you need to spice them up with accessories and color. Make room for color and lively clothing that reflect a woman who is loved and loves herself also.

There is something natural to dancing to praise music. King David in Psalms danced before the Lord often. He was joyful and wanted to praise God and dance was just a part of it. Children seem to know that dance is pure and a part of a happy life. A free spirit dances. Go ahead and dance. Even if someone is watching, they may want to join in too! There actually are garments you can purchase for praise worshiping and praise dancing. Check it out online.

Journal page for chapter eleven, Dancing Clothes

On this page write down what you learned about praise. How will you show Him praise? Only on a Sunday? Will you praise Him all week long no matter where you are? How can choosing joy in your life bring you out of your mourning? List as many things that you have learned so far in this book that give you a reason for praising God and Jesus.

You are a Gift

We all love to receive gifts, especially at birthdays, holidays and on special occasions. Gifts come in different, shall we say, "Packages." Homemade, store bought, coupons for services, gift cards, money cards, and more. Children are a gift from God to the family. Loving others is a gift. A smile to a stranger is a gift.

I was wanting a set of dishes in the collection of "the Twelve days of Christmas," but I couldn't afford them. Inwardly I was hoping to find anything that would be in that style. One day my husband and I went on a trip and along the way we decided to stray off the beaten path and explore the small local shops. We stopped at a rummage sale and I saw some cookie cutters in a bag. I collect cookie cutters so I was excited. But not as excited as I was when I got home and realized I had a complete set of Twelve Days of Christmas cookie cutters! What a special gift from God that was to me!

We don't often think of gifts in a broader sense, like the gift of life, donating organs or blood, until we or someone close to us has a need. The Word of God reveals to us spiritual gifts such as; the *gifts* of healing, prophesy, words of knowledge, teaching and speaking in other tongues. There are the daily gifts we get from God: the gift of breath, health, safe passage to and from destinations, relationships, a second, third or fourth chance to make things right. The gift of time we give to others. We may never know what we were all spared from just having our day altered by a few minutes. We take the gifts of God for granted. Sometimes we misunderstand what God is doing in our lives and we need clarity. Take a moment to consider these with me:

What or *who* has God said no to, off limits about? THE GIFT *is the no*; keep looking for God's perfect plan. He knows the best for us, he sees the future, trust Him alone.

What is it that He has gifted you with? Start with "HE IS THE GIFT." Then, follow that with sharing your talents and gifts with your family, friends and the rest of us.

What are you doing with the spiritual gifts He gave you? USE THEM IN FAITH. Don't hide them from the world like I have in the past.

Are you living out the destiny that God has planned for you? THE GIFT *is the Designed plan for your life*. Oh, and it is a gift. He has planned so many good things for you.

Often times we only see what we want to see. We don't realize we are not ready for some things or it is not good for us to know everything. God's perfect timing and our best interests are His *first priority*. I wanted so desperately to know everything about some abusive situations that had happened to me as a child. I was even tempted to go see a hypnotist. I couldn't remember everything but as I got older I began reacting to so many things that I knew there were more things that had happened. That is what PTSD is like, you just don't remember everything all at once, nor at the same time.

Recently I found out more information and it just made me want to know more. Why? I really don't know, I guess maybe for what I thought would be closure. It wasn't until recently that I have been working on my reactions to people and events and am learning that gifts come in many packages. I realized He GIFTED ME by *not* letting me know what all had happened to me. There is even a scripture for that.

Isaiah 51:16

"I have covered thee in the shadow of mine hand."

I need to remember a sinner chose to sin and it had happened and God sheltered me in it. God chose to gift me with memory loss of those incidents. I had a head injury and still suffer from short term memory. I hated every time I would forget something. I felt incomplete, empty and fearful of what might happen if I got lost or couldn't remember my own name. I already forgot other's names and places. I had to learn to trust Him to make it through many things, including getting home, when I forgot where I lived. If you had asked me then, if memory loss was a good thing, I would not have agreed with you. I have accepted that He is in control of my life and *if I will* trust Him He will complete me and help me to fulfill my destiny. His plan for me didn't end when the bad things happened to me. It was just postponed until He had a chance to heal me and make me wholly His.

Are you thankful for the gifts He has given you? I am very thankful for the gifts He has given me, including the gift of friendships. The gift of words of encouragement. Here are some for you!

YOU ARE A GIFT from GOD,
to your family and friends, those in your circle of life.
YOU ARE A GIFT to GOD,
He delights in your very existence, like a loving father does.
YOU ARE A GIFT TO THE WORLD,
your life will touch others in many ways.
YOU HAVE A DESTINY,
a plan for your talents to be used for the benefit of all of us.
YOUR *LIFE* IS JUST BEGINNING,
the future is brighter than ever, keep focus on it.

[For more scriptures on the gifts refer to the appendix]

Closet purging time for, You are a Gift

This is another chapter where I ask you not to purge but to add something to your closet. Do you like gifts? Well, I do. I want you to make one for your closet. Take a piece of paper, write <u>your name</u> on it. You can make it special by doing calligraphy or just simply print it. Then take that paper and put it in an envelope, on the outside of the envelope write <u>Christ Jesus</u>. Then take that envelope, no need to lick it shut, and put it in a beautifully decorated box. Put a tag on it that says <u>God the Father</u>. Now, what you have is this. YOU are in Christ Jesus, who is in the Father God. You are in HIM and in God.

You are the gift.

Journal page for chapter twelve, You are a Gift

For this chapter I want you to focus on the gifts that God has given you, the gift of family, health, wisdom, dreams, laughter, anything that brings blessings to you or others first. Now, list all those that come to your mind that *you* give to God, others or to yourself. And finally, list all the small gifts along the way you that have received from others, whether it is spiritual, physical, emotional, words of encouragement are gifts also. What did you learn about yourself from this chapter? What can you offer as a gift? What hidden gifts do you have? What is your favorite type of gift?

Your Glorious Destiny

You've been given a great destiny from God to complete.
You alone can do it and no one else can match it.

I like to refer to God as being our designer, but let's expand it to "God our Travel agent." Travel agent you say? Well, don't you think a destiny has a destination? Oh yeah sister, get those suitcases ready because God has a travel plan for YOU! You won't be sitting on the sidelines where His plan for you is concerned. No way! Your head may spin and your heart may tremble, He is full of exciting adventures.

YOU *are a unique Gift from God to the World.*
Your Talents will honor God, bless others and satisfy your soul.

While He is my Creator, he also gave me talents to create. At the age of nine, I was already sewing by hand and making my own doll clothes and doll houses out of cardboard boxes, making curtains and decorating the rooms. I even created my own stuffed Snoopy dog, without a pattern. It was pretty good too! I was sewing clothing by age twelve and making my own designs and fashions. By the time I was in high school, I was known for saying, "I could've made it cheaper." Later on I was told I put a little "Tweety" (myself) in everything I make. I love to embellish. Creating is fun, I still love it. I had wanted to become a fashion designer, but I was not secure in myself to go after it. I do still design a little for my own purposes. There are some days I regret I didn't follow through in being in the fashion industry.

It is so very true; no one else can fulfill your destiny. Unfortunately, many never fulfill their destiny due to unbelief, fears and lack of confidence in themselves. I have experienced all of those. If you are reading this book it proves first, that there *is* a God and next that He *fulfills* all that HE promises to do in us. He helped me to overcome my doubts and fears. If you had asked me if I was going to write a book a few years ago, I would have said, "Me? What, no way! I'm not good at anything." Okay, maybe talking. That is, now anyway. When I was a child and into my teens, actually into my early twenties, I was so very shy I didn't really talk to a lot of people.

God has a way of getting me to talk even though I still have a nervous rash and blotchy red skin while I'm talking, or teaching others. Now I love to talk and share with others. After meeting someone in a store and briefly talking to them, they often times share some personal stories with me, whether it's about their children or something else. My husband will come up and say, "Oh, do you know them?" I'd answer, "No, just met them." He'd be so astonished. He wondered how on earth someone would be so open with me in such a short time. I tell him it's because I pose absolutely no threat to anyone, I'm so nice of course! Sometimes I actually feel like we would've made good friends and I should've asked for their number!

I like to look at this book as my "one to one" conversation with you, my new friend, journeying together in our friendship, as most friends do, helping one another through the tough times of life. I know, I know. I'm not there physically for you. Like the scarf that someone made for me, a wounded woman, (mentioned in the Accessories chapter). Although I may never know who made it, I'll never forget that **someone** was thinking of me, caring and wanting to share something with me. Maybe they have even prayed for me. I wear that scarf with a sense of attachment to the one who made it. I matter, I am worthy, and I exist to someone. So do you. I'm hoping this book helps, because you do matter, exist, have value and purpose also. You were in my thoughts and prayers as I wrote these words.

On with our chapter. We don't choose our own destiny. God has already planned it out for us! In the scriptures God says, "I knew you in your mother's womb, knit YOU together, formed you." So that means that God formed you from the top of the little hairs on your head to the tip of your little toes, not to mention all the brain functions and character traits, all your little intricacies and talents, even the way you walk, male or female. Whether you will be athletic or musical, artistic or professionally inclined, God put into you all that you were going to need to fulfill His perfect plan. All while you were growing in your mother's womb.

What does that have to do with destiny? Plenty, destiny is what you fulfill using your gifts, talents, wisdom, strengths, physical and mental capabilities to their fullest. That does mean work, schooling, training, practice, obedience to His word.

The dictionary lists destiny as: "the fate, or fortune, for which a person is destined; their lot in life; the preordained or predetermined ordering of events." It's a noun. Which means it's a real thing, not a perception or dream or thought. Thankfully, God has made one for each of us. We don't have to leave it to chance or fate or someone else's views or plans for us. Since He made us, who better to create the path we are to take. Sure, we get off track or run amuck some days, but we are always able to get back on the path of our destiny. The only way to know your destiny is to follow the path set before you. How do you do that?

Take a good look at your abilities, desires and your dreams. What do others tell you that you are good at? What is your passion? Maybe you have more than one. I know I do. As a kid I sewed a lot. I drew sketchbook pads full of Avon containers my aunt had at her house. I am pretty decent at crafting and make attempts at decorating as well. Recently I created small hats to bless my friends with at a church ladies outing. I wanted to be a fashion designer, that is, until I saw the shows and saw how stressful it looks. Maybe that is my own fear. I loved kids and always wanted to be a foster or adopted parent. I don't think I did too badly with my own kids. They still like me and we enjoy each other's company.

There is a saying, "Plan your work and work your plan." What that means is, you have to plan, make arrangements, and say yes to new things and no to things that keep you from completing your goals. I'm not saying here that you should ignore family members or their needs. Marriage and children may be a part of our destiny but not the whole of it. It begins with us changing our inner thoughts and then changing our actions, motivations and decisions. I can't tell you what yours is, but it will follow God's Word, the Bible. Pray and ask God what He has in store for you!

Proverbs 31 is a good place to start. (*You can find the whole scripture in the appendix*) If we take apart this scripture we find a great deal of insight for a designed destiny.

She is valuable. She realized her value, got motivated to rise above her limitations and negative thoughts to have a glorious future. (I'm hoping you do too by now, not because I said so but because it's true.)

She is trustworthy. That means she lives a life of honesty and truth in every area of her life. She is good to others, not harming anyone. Others have put their trust in her.

She is safe to be around. She wanted to be around those who supported and encouraged her, those who protect her heart, mind and soul. Those who nourish others.

She creates something marketable. She shops at Hobby Lobby and makes things. No, it doesn't say that exactly, haa haa. She considers her talents, whether its business related, family orientated, ministry related or other gifts. Her efforts were necessary to accomplish it. That meant she needed to trust and be more assertive and aggressively move forward on each project.

She brings her food from afar. She isn't stuck with boring food choices, she creates food that enhances her health and seeks new things to try. She shops for sales, value and variety.

She considers the needs of others. She plans ahead for weather, health, and spiritual needs of her family. She joins groups like school council, charity organizations and other groups to assist others in their needs.

She is business savvy. She considers business deals. She uses her *God given* wisdom, makes her decisions and buys the land. She proceeds to plant a vineyard, which will bring in money and also give jobs to others.

She gains strength and exercises. Yes really, it says that. She realizes it's important to take time to keep her health and strength up so she can do all that is required of her and it also reduces stress. I could use a bit more of that!

She sees value in her talent and works diligently in it. She had talent and used her abilities and marketed the products. She didn't waste her purpose on temporal things. She saw the value she had in her abilities and went for it. She had nothing to lose, but all to gain.

She works hard with her hands. She is motivated and doesn't give up, but continues in her work because she knows it is a good thing. She didn't give up if became difficult or challenging. She knew a challenge was a good thing. She focused on the challenge and was motivated and encouraged in her good works, talents and abilities.

She considers the needy. She is community conscious, caring for those who cannot care for themselves. She knows it is so important to know her neighbors and care for the people in her community. She knows that we all affect each other.

She doesn't worry when winter comes. She is *prepared* for the weathering elements. She prepares for bad weather with proper clothing, whether hot or cold. More than that, she is prepared for life's little, or big, bumps along the way. She knows that by planning ahead for the unforeseen events, be it financial or physical or spiritual or emotional, she is not only spared the hardship, but the emotional trauma too. She stays close to the One who can lead her through those things, namely, the Lord God.

She wears fine clothing. She is fashion savvy and dresses herself in fashionable clothes. She shops at thrift stores, no one in her home wears rags. She tries new things.

Her husband has a position of authority. She didn't choose the guy who refused to work, or the one who did drugs, nor was lazy. She chose a mate who was *honorable*. He was a vital part of their community. This is a serious topic. We need to choose good mates. The saying goes, chose a date that would make a good mate. No sense wasting your time on a guy who isn't husband material if you plan on marriage one day.

She also makes fine linen garments and sells them. She considers the trend of the current market. Linen was the majority of clothing choices for garments at that time, and sashes were always needed. She was aware of the trends and possibilities in her time of history. She knew she may have the answer to a flawed plan, a design to a problem or a song for the brokenhearted. The simplest of things can be overlooked and she knew her wisdom may be just what was needed at that time.

She will rejoice in time to come. Strength and honor are her clothing. She may feel a bit overwhelmed now, but will, in time, rejoice because she was steadfast in the work of her hands and mind. When she gathers the produce that has grown over the summer and wash and prepare it for canning, she does so every year because she can rejoice in knowing she made it, and she has saved money too.

She opens her mouth with wisdom and speaks words of kindness. She was strong enough to use godly wisdom, found in the Word, such as here in Proverbs. She spoke kind words to others. She spoke from her heart and she choose her words carefully.

She pays attention to the needs of her house. No bon bons for her. She isn't lazy, she cares for her home, whether it's cleaning or caring for her family, raising her children and meeting the needs of her husband. She pays attention and recognizes what each member needs to fulfill their life's destiny also. She knows her children's abilities. She will guide them to their natural talents and God-given destiny.

She is blessed and praised by her family. Her family is so thankful for her attention to their needs that they feel loved and call her blessed. Her husband praises her. She is a strong individual who completely found her destiny, and didn't lose the family along the way doing it. She knows she won't be perfect, but does her best every day.

Many women have done well, but you exceed them all. She is now enjoying her life, having accomplished what she set out to do. She feels completed and whole. Managing and fulfilling her dreams through hard work and patience and perseverance. She knows this isn't a competition, but still wants to do well.

She seeks Godly approval first. No sweet voice or pretty face will replace the true value of a woman, but a woman who fears the Lord, will be praised. If she may had the Wisdom of Solomon, the beauty of Esther, but didn't follow God's plan, she wouldn't be victorious, nor have the proper focus. She didn't seek beauty as an end, she sought God and was beautiful inside and it shown outwardly.

She is known by the works she does. Give her the fruit of her hands, and let her own works praise her in the gates. She will have a legacy of her own right when she fulfills her own destiny. She will have her reward whether in finances, relationships, marketable items, designs, etc.

Did you find yourself anywhere in those verses? Look deeper and see where you fit in. I understand not all will be married, nor have children. The focus here isn't family as much as it is having direction and developing motivation. Use your physical and emotional strength to persevere till you reach our goals. Now is a good time to make some goals, don't make it a pressure thing, you can have fun with it. I'm learning to walk out my destiny just like you are doing.

You can do this. It is more fun to do it together, get a group of friends and family to help you realize your talents. Hopefully you have begun to unload your old emotional suitcases, so now you can begin preparing for your lifelong spiritual journey. Remember to read the Word of God and pray. Your life will unfold, and become whole, healed inside and then your journey will begin outward. Then He can move you to where you need to go and fulfill your destiny. It may be global, or just across the street. You may fly or walk or run in a marathon. I remember watching the movie, "Chariots of Fire" and being very motivated. The opportunities are endless. Be ready!

Closet purging time for,
Your Glorious Destiny

If you were going on a journey you would take things of necessity, maybe a few frivolous things, but mainly the things you actually would wear and need. For this chapter, I want you to first purge your closet from all things that don't belong in a closet. We all have some stuff in there we are just storing or hiding, don't we. Then, I want you to consider the other items in your closet that you haven't worn in over a year. I'm not talking about costumes or holiday evening wear. Those are used occasionally and may be kept if, first of all they fit and second of all if they are appropriate for a new you! Look carefully and go through the closet from top to bottom. Toss or send to thrift store, don't look back.

Our trip needs to be a joyous one, no extra baggage wearing us down. Too much stuff wears us down. We have to clean around it and keep moving it all the time. I'll bet you find stuff in there you never thought you had. Down memory lane? Find a way to keep the memories without all the stuff. Oh, and dust off your luggage. You never know when or where your destiny will take you.

Journal page for chapter thirteen, Your Glorious Destiny

I would like you to write on this page your "bucket list." You know, the one you make of all things you wanted to do or places you always wanted to go see before you kick the "proverbial bucket." Then make a list of all your talents and abilities that God put in you for us, the world. Do any of them match up? Where do you see yourself in 5 years from now? What steps can you take today, this week, plans you can make to begin your God given destiny? Cleaning out our emotional and physical closets open us up for new things, clothes as well as opportunities. Don't miss out on the best life you will ever have.

Shield of Faith

What do you have in your closet that you have used as a form of protection in the past? When I think of a shield, I think of it protecting one thing from another. People use many different types of shielding. We use coats to shield us from the cold, umbrellas to shield us from the rain. We use sunscreen and sunglasses to shield us from the sun's harmful rays. We use lip balm to shield our lips from the drying winter air. We are so vulnerable, we are in constant need of something, other than ourselves, to shield us from just about everything. We don't have in ourselves many means of protection or shielding. Face it, we need something, or someone, to be that for us. The shield of faith is not something we can live without. It is a must have for every believer. We are at war with our Father God's enemy, satan. The enemy is always ready to make trouble with and for us.

Harmful Shields of the flesh:

First, let's talk about how we use the wrong type of shield. I'll call them the shields of the flesh. We use the wrong shields when we use our own thinking, or quick actions, before we take time to think clearly, or pray, about something we encounter in our lives. We **use our words in defense** against others, using anger to push someone away that we perceive is getting to close or may be prying into our personal space or lives. Maybe they are too close to the truth about us, but we don't want to admit it. We say things that hurt others so they leave us alone. Some even use the knowledge of personal information about someone else as an offering to others, to spare themselves being the next victim of gossip or targeting. Thinking we have shielded ourselves, we have actually set ourselves up for backlash. Scripture says our sin will find us out. Eventually, the truth comes out and we have to face the consequences of our actions. No one wins on that one.

We use **lies as a shield**, afraid of being known for our real self. We lie to others about who we are, thinking no one would want us if they knew who we really are. We lie to ourselves, saying "I'll never get that job, a husband, a child, or a house, so why try." **Being overweight is not a shield from harm**. *It is you harming yourself*. There is no protection, you may feel rejected, but *first by you*. We overeat to shield ourselves from rejection, lying to ourselves that no one would want us anyway. You reject your female self and hide behind layers of unhealthy weight gain. You reject your destiny and make your own unhealthy path. You reject God's design for you as a woman worthy of accomplishing great things. You are worthy of being loved and giving love.

Don't worry about those who will feel bad when you become the best you can be. They are only jealous, if they can't rejoice with you and your successes, they really aren't friends

73

then are they? Let's all rejoice with each other and begin our path of healthy lifestyle choices. Enjoy treating yourself to the healthy weight you were meant to be.

We think that by becoming overweight we will protect ourselves from further danger of sexual abuse. When all along we are in danger of our own emotional breakdown and physical harm to our own healthy future.

We *put up walls physically and emotionally* to shield ourselves from harmful situations, events, memory of events and often time's people, who may or may not hurt us. Since my abuser was bald, I confess I have a hard time not putting up walls when I see any older bald man. Sorry to admit it. My "spidey" senses go up and I can't ignore the fact that it reminds me of that person and I am fearful and distrusting of that stereotype. I know in my mind it is irrelevant. There are a lot of older men who are bald who would never do such a thing, but in my subconscious I am still working it out. I am not as trusting as I'd like. I cannot allow myself to be automatically judgmental of them. I know, *I know,* they can't help it if they go bald. In *my mind,* I am shielding myself from any harm by not allowing myself to trust any bald guy, initially. Perhaps your shield goes up when you see anyone who reminds you of your abuser.

God wants to be our shield. The words of David the Psalmist who loved and served God are this:

Psalms 115:11
"You that fear the LORD, trust in the LORD: He *is* your help and your shield."

Psalms 5:12
"For you, LORD, will bless the righteous;
With *favor you will compass him with a shield.*"

Psalms 3:3
"But *you, O LORD, are a shield for me*; my glory, and the lifter up of my head."

Think of these verses when you are mistreated by others, including your co—workers. He puts people in positions when and where He wants to. He promotes and demotes. He exalts and raises up. He changes the hearts of "kings", employers, family members, neighbors and etc. No one is out of his realm of influence of change.

Ephesians 6:16
"Above all, taking the shield of faith, wherein
you shall be able to quench all the fiery darts of the wicked."

What more fiery darts are there but that which comes from the mouth? People can be so harmful when they want to be. The written word in emails, Facebook and Twitter can ruin someone's reputation in a nano second. No taking it back either. Ever hear of the story of the feather pillow? Rip one open and throw it all outside a window. Now try to gather all of the feathers, not leaving any. It is impossible. So are hurtful words.

Healthy Shields of faith:

Now, let's talk about the good healthy shields. The ones that really give us what we really need. There are many people who used shields of faith in the Bible. A shield of faith means, **we put our faith in front of us**. Make sure faith goes before our fears, physical strengths or disabilities in the face of warfare, spiritual or physical. Hebrews chapter 11 also talks about faith. Check out some of the people who used their faith shields.

David used his shield of faith <u>as trust in God's strength</u> to conquer the giant, killing the enemy of God. As a sheepherder, he had to fight the bears and lions. To him that Philistine would be as one of them, conquerable. His faith made him a force to be reckoned with. (For more information see 1 Samuel chapter 17)

Deborah used her shield of faith to lead men to war. She was a prophetess who discerned and prophesied God's word to the people. She was born to help deliver God's people from their enemy. Barak would not lead the army without her presence. He trusted in her faith. Her shield was her faith in God <u>to show to her what she needed for wisdom and discernment for the people in and out of battle</u>. She judged the nation for over forty years after the war was won. She used God's wisdom and the spoken word from God to lead the army to victory. Find the whole story in Judges, Chapters 4 and 5.

Mary used her shield of faith as she <u>*obeyed the words of God through an angel, in spite of rejection from family and society.*</u> Her culture called for death of one who was unmarried and pregnant. Even though it came from the angel to carry in her womb the Savior of the World, she would be mocked, made fun of and worst of all labeled a woman of no morals. Everyone would think she slept around. A virgin no longer in their eyes. Unclean. Shunned. She may have lost friends and family trust. Yet she held her shield with the strength of God during her pregnancy and throughout her life. Read more about Mary in Luke chapters 1–3.

Daniel used his shield of faith <u>*in putting his life on the line. He would only serve and honor God alone.*</u> He trusted God to spare him from power driven men who put him in with hungry lions in the pit. God shielded him from the lions eating him. His life was spared because he believed and would not change his life for others, no matter who they were. No matter what manner of death he might have encountered, he was not going to bow to any other god, nor man. Find out why he needed God's help in Daniel chapter 3.

Stephen used his shield of faith as he forgave those who murdered him as they were stoning him. <u>*He did not allow the pain*</u> (of the rocks nor the pain of knowing someone wanted him dead) <u>*to penetrate his spiritual body*</u>, <u>*his shield protected him from that*</u> pain as *he trusted that his faith in God was stronger than the evil around him.* God's provision for him in heaven was worth the short painful persecuted death that was occurring to him at the time. He knew it was eternity with God that mattered. May God grant us all that kind of faith! Read more about the disciples in the book of Acts.

Esther, using her shield of faith, left protocol, to enter the court unannounced, nor summoned by her husband the King, when it meant sudden death to do so. It also could've meant banishment from her husband and her position as Queen, just as Vashti, her predecessor was. She now collected her <u>*courage from her faith in her God*</u> that had put her in the palace at just that time in history for the purpose of saving her people, the Jews from annihilation from their enemies. She hadn't told anyone of her Jewish heritage as of yet. She went and asked for the safety of her people, that they would be able to defend themselves. They were saved by her courageous actions. For more on this story you can read the book of Esther.

Jesus is our shield from satan and hell. How you ask? He took the blows so we don't have to. We didn't deserve Jesus doing that. God loved us that much. ***He is also a shield from the storms of life***, from our own consequences. He is a shield from our own selfish ways, and the continual emotional damage from the harm of others, when we let Him in our lives.

Ephesians 6:16
**"Above all, taking the shield of faith,
So you will be able to quench all the fiery darts of the wicked."**

A good warrior acknowledges and studies his enemy. The word of God tells us about our enemy, satan, the devil. Don't study the enemy as to *know* him, but to know the ways he will attack you. Look up the word of God and read the accounts of satans tactics. Use the word as a shield thwarting satans vile attempts to harm you.

The warrior's shield was wetted down and soaked through so it could extinguish the fire from the darts. If we are soaked in God's word when, not if, the fiery words of others or negative thoughts come, we can easily squelch them, before they cause us emotional harm. I have a toy shield and I use it to remind myself I need to use the spiritual word of God as my shield more often. Maybe you could do the same.

Come and fight the good fight with me as my comrades in the faith. Together we can build an arsenal against the enemy. We will help each other to hold up our shields and if need be you can find shelter behind mine until you are strong enough to carry your own. There is rejoicing after the battle. I read the end of the story, WE WIN!

Closet purging time for, Shield of Faith

With this chapter, I want you to dig deep. Since I mentioned we use clothing to cover up our true selves, I want you to go into your closet and look for the clothes that you have used to hide under. The clothing that is too big, or too small, maybe you didn't want to admit you've gained weight. Look for clothing that really doesn't fit into your new look, a woman of excellence. Get rid of those things that don't compliment your shape or your weight. You want to wear clothes that are attractive, not distractive or distasteful. Keep your faith in Christ and in what He will do for you and through you. You won't need to hide under clothing when you have Him lovingly guiding and supporting you.

Journal page for chapter fourteen, Shield of Faith

I want you to be really honest with yourself and list all the shields you have used in your past that you thought would protect you from something or someone. Take your time and list as many as you can. It will help you understand a lot about yourself if you do. After reading this chapter, what will you use in the future to protect you from harm? What faith lessons did you learn from this chapter?

Lipstick

You are probably wondering what could possibly be spiritual about lipstick. Haa haa. Well, our mouths are what we use to speak words. Our words affect our own lives and those around us. Our words can make or break relationships. We can use words to build up or tear down, either ourselves or others. When I was a new Christian, I had to make changes to represent Christ in my speech also.

Ephesians 4:22
"That ye *put off concerning the former conversation* the old man,
which is corrupt according to the deceitful lusts."

I am by nature a fixer. Maybe you are too. So I get involved more than I should when I see things that are not what they should be. I have to decide to **act, not react** to what happens around me. I need to remember that everyone's emotional state is not my fault, nor is it my duty to fix them. I just need to take a step back and be calm. Assess the situation, pray and ask for wisdom to handle it, doing unto others, what I want done to me and not to sow discord.

James 3:2, 8-10, NIV Version
"For we all stumble in many ways.
If anyone is never at fault in what he says, he is a perfect man,
able to keep his whole body in check.
But no one can tame the tongue *it is* a restless evil, full of deadly poison.
With the tongue, we praise our Lord and Father; and with it, we curse men,
who are made in God's likeness.
Out of the same mouth comes praise and cursing.
My brothers this should not be."

I need to watch what I say about those who have hurt me. By sharing how I was hurt, I was inadvertently giving a negative slant and even though it was true, the only thing the hearers got was the negative characteristics of that person. I need to focus on the positive characteristics they have instead of only the negative ones. I need to look at those events that made me angry or hurt and see what I needed to do to be assertive yet polite, and what to ignore from other's behavior. I need to have on a shield to absorb the fiery darts others shoot at me. I can bless them with God's grace and love. Finally, if I can't say anything good, then I need to say nothing at all about them. I am not saying you cannot talk to anyone. Find a pastor, counselor or a godly friend to discuss your painful issues. Do pray together about it. Sometimes just hearing ourselves talk about it, gives us the answers we need to know.

My mouth deceives me when I get angry over situations. My heart is full of raw emotion and my words tell others more than I think they do. When I cannot get over a situation and keep repeating it, my heart says it is not satisfied. Whatever is in our hearts comes out in our words. Good or bad. Our words reveal our hearts intent. When I *remember* to ask God to put a guard on my mouth, He is faithful to do just that. He keeps me from using my own emotional state in my words to others.

Matthew 12:34b says,
"For out of the abundance of the heart the mouth speaks."

Remember, our words have an effect on us, if we say we can't do anything, we won't try. If we say we can, we will make every effort to do it. Using positive words of faith will get us through more than complaining about it. Others tell me to speak the word of God, not my own feelings on a matter. This is a weak area for me. I tend to just look at the immediate truth and not see what Gods view is in it. I need to slow down and use scripture to determine my actions and words.

We also need to consider our own self-talk. What are you saying about yourself? Do you have a healthy self-image? Do you talk down about yourself often? It is one thing to acknowledge you have done something wrong, but to continually cut yourself down verbally to yourself or to others sends a message that you are not worth anything. Self-doubt about your abilities or about your worth is harmful to a healthy life. It will keep you from being your best, drag you down and suffocate you, so don't do it. Practice daily saying at least one thing you do like about yourself aloud and be sincere.

Lipsticks do have an expiration date. We need to remember to throw out old thoughts and forget negative words from others. On the other hand, our negative words give others a bad taste in their mouth about us also. Let's try to keep fresh words that are positive in our hearts. Renewing your mind with God's word daily will give you a positive focus for you and others.

Philippians 4:8
"Finally, brethren, whatever things are true, whatever things *are* honest, whatever things *are* just, whatsoever things *are* pure, and whatsoever things *are* lovely, whatever things *are* of good report; if *there be* any virtue, and if *there be* any praise, think on these things."

Closet purging time for, Lipstick

Yes, even this chapter has a purging. If you have any old makeup now is the time to remove it. This is good for several reasons. One, old makeup carries germs, e coli germs as well. Two, you probably aren't using the old colors anymore. Try some of the newer make up that has fewer chemicals in them. It is always a good reminder never to share your make up as it does spread germs. Mascara is usually only good for three months before it develops germs. Since it is for the eye area better safe than sorry!

Journal pages for chapter fifteen,
Lipstick

Write down all the hurtful things that seem to keep rearing their ugly heads in your conversations. Who is it about? What did they do, or not do, to cause you sorrow? What does God's word say about the situation? Can you or will you forgive them? Maybe you need a mediator to assist you in talking to the person. Do it soon. Anger turns to bitterness, which turns into resentment, which is harder to get rid of.

Personal Fashion Designer, God

Every clothing brand has a designer. Those of you who watch the fashion shows or the runways will recognize the name, Vera Wang. Even the celebrities are making clothing styles of their own. Maybe you've even dreamed of becoming a fashion designer. In this book, I refer to God as **our personal fashion designer.** He is more than a designer of clothes, He has personally designed each one of us to make a difference in this world.

In this section, I'd like to introduce you to God by telling you who He is to me. When I was born, God was my Creator. He created me in my mother's womb. In my childhood, I only heard He was God, the awesome, fearful man upstairs. I was afraid of disobeying Him and being disciplined by Him. I wanted to obey, but only to save my soul. I really did not *know* Him. I was afraid of being sent to Hell. That fear kept me from getting into trouble, but not enough to save me.

I was nine the summer my dad died. My friend invited me to her church Bible camp for a week. They talked about salvation and I accepted Jesus into my heart. Upon returning to the Catholic Church, I was quickly confused, since they didn't talk about a personal relationship with God or Jesus. So I just went on trying in my own strength to be a good person.

At fifteen years old, the Lord gave me a friend who asked me to her non-denominational church and this time I understood what I was doing and Jesus became my personal savior. I received strength, wisdom, and direction from Him. He helped me stay sexually pure in an impure world. I was teased for my faith, and was called a Jesus freak. I told them that Jesus takes freaks and makes people out of them, not the other way around. He protected me from further harmful situations.

I married at age twenty and got pregnant four months later. I experienced two miscarriages in six months and was so heartbroken that I prayed and asked God for twins to replace them. One month later, I was pregnant. God knows the sorrows we have and helps us through them. In my fourth month of pregnancy I was previously scheduled to go to a seminar for women, called, "What happens when women pray." I had my ultrasound the day before and found out we were having twins. I shared my faith story with the ladies and their faith was increased as a result.

Months later, when the girls were two months old, I was carrying one of them and was about to go down the stairs. My foot was already off the top landing and I was nearly propelled to go down the steps falling with the baby when all of a sudden something miraculously pushed my foot up hard enough for me to get back on the landing. I should've fallen down the steps with the baby. I am convinced it was the hand of God. He protected us from injury.

He has been my protection from car accidents. I prayed over vehicles that were not quite suitable for the road and one day while I drove one, I ran out of gas. It was on the highway and it happened that God put me right where a man was tending his garden. I walked over to him and he helped me get gasoline. The gas gauge did not work and I hadn't known I was that low. I made it home and two hours later, the whole back end of the vehicle dropped down, and all that had happened to me was I ran out of gas. God had spared us from an accident on the highway.

Another time I prayed over a different car that had a funny noise. I had been to town and was returning home when I lost control of the steering wheel and something loudly dropped from the engine. I swerved from the left to right sides of the road. There were at least three vehicles that were in the oncoming traffic that I should've hit. A semi-truck and two cars. I don't know how we were spared from that! I had crossed the line several times without hitting one of them! I finally made it across to the right shoulder and a strange peace came over me. We were not only safe, but within walking distance of our home.

There was a time when we had very little money and ate lentils for protein for a whole week, because we couldn't afford meat. Lentil meatloaf, lentil soup, lentil hamburgers, there is only so much lentils you can eat and still make interesting. I was sitting down to the lentil soup wondering if I should eat bread with my soup or save it for a sandwich the next day. I decided to eat the bread and trust God to feed us. Suddenly the doorbell rang and when my husband opened the door there were three bags of groceries and they even remembered my birthday with a card. I may not have always had food I enjoyed but I have never gone hungry.

One time we needed car repairs but had no finances to get them done. I had just paid the bills and there wasn't even enough money for much food either. I paid my church tithe and prayed that God would meet our needs. The very next day after church, my husband sat down in the car seat and realized he sat on something. It was an envelope with money. Not only was there enough for car repairs and food, but also enough for me to see a doctor. I had pneumonia so it covered that and my medication as well. God sent someone to be His hands in our time of need.

During a time when I was deeply depressed, I was driving somewhere with the girls, a voice said, "Drive into that lake and drown yourself." I was so very sad and lonely and empty inside, but I would never harm my children. I kept on driving and I realized that the voice came from satan. I know God has had his hand on me, pulling me through all these trials and temptations. One day at a time.

Years later, I had just finished my devotions and was trying to fall asleep when I saw a man in pants and white shirt come through the window. My bedroom is on the second story. I tried in vain to wake my husband, shaking him and everything, but he wouldn't wake up. It was like a dream but I was awake. Instantly I was wrestling with the spirit, struggling and calling out "Jesus help me," several times. He left nearly as quickly as he came, just like poof, gone. Then I heard a voice say, "Do not fear men."

A few months after that I went to my mom's house and didn't get home till after midnight. There was a known sexual deviant in the neighborhood and as I got out of the car I saw he was walking from one building to his home. Unfortunately for me, I also had to go that way to get to my apartment. I tried to hurry and as I walked he came closer and closer. I nearly screamed, but he passed me as though he never saw me. I felt the breeze of his passing, he nearly ran into me. I know that God protected me that night.

God has been *designing* my life and *making alterations* for me all along the way. For instance, when I was putting off writing this book, God sent three individuals on different occasions to tell me I was procrastinating. They didn't know what I was supposed to do, but I did. It was not a rebuke as much as a gentle reminder, He gave me the book to write for Him, not of my own accord but from Him.

I had acted like an adopted kid. Never trusting in anyone. However, He has shown himself faithful in more and more things so that I can't help but trust Him. He has seen me through bad stuff, my children's sorrows, and grief in relationships. He has kept me from adultery when I was lonely. I didn't want to sin against God. Since I was faithful, He was faithful to me. Faith encourages faith, keep building on it.

He has been my peace and comfort in weary emotional times. Strength when I wanted to check out of this world. Endurance to finish the race of this journey. If He can bring me through all this, He can do the same and so much more for you and your situation.

Some of us don't have a father's arms to run to. Or do we? Last time I checked, we still do have a father to run to, God the Father, God our Father. Man may give us his genes but God gives us life. He has given me the ability to teach children. He has given me talents in sewing, crafts, and managing a household. He blessed me with children, a spouse who is faithful. He has given me compassion for others. He is sharing with me His wisdom for this book so I can share His heart with you. His heart is only good towards you, never bad. He breathes life into us. He is Life. He is peace and health and love. All that is good is God. So we can't stand in judgment of Him and say, "You did this to me," when He isn't evil. He is only and always good. He seeks only "good" for us. After all is said and done, no matter what happens to us, there is no other God but Him. His designs are meticulous, functional and practical, you won't be disappointed with His results.

He alone is worthy of our worship, praise, and honor.

Closet purging time for, Personal Fashion Designer, God

You are probably wondering what in the world do I have in my closet that I need to purge that has to do with God. The clothing industry has made t-shirts and sweatshirts and other garments, tennis shoes, jewelry and even hair accessories using printed skulls, and other types of morally unsuitable things for clothing. The skull is a symbol of death. If we are to put our lives in the hands of a Living God, why would we want to parade ourselves around wearing death? If we want to have others speak good words to us, why would we wear garments defaming others?

Let's think for a moment. Who are we representing? What do we really want others to think about us? All I ask is that you pray about it. Maybe you disagree with me. If you agree with me, please see if you have anything that is of any satanic origin, negative words or pictures and rid your closet and your home of them.

Journal page for chapter sixteen, Personal Fashion Designer, God

On this page I'd like for you to write down your past knowledge or experience of who God is. Maybe you've never heard of Him, or maybe He wasn't portrayed very well to you by someone else's actions or beliefs. Or by the influence of others' disbeliefs. Write down what you think of Him yourself. Good, bad, anything you feel is what I want you to write down. This is your journal. Did this chapter change your view in any way? How so? Have you seen God in your life lately? Something in your life that only God could've done for you?

Our Spiritual Wardrobe, The Armor of God

I live in Wisconsin. It gets *really* cold here in the winter. Brrrrr. I wear several layers. I never know if I'll get stuck somewhere or have to stand outside very long. I had an old heavy pigskin winter coat with hood that has fake fur inside. It was the warmest coat I've ever had. It wasn't the prettiest coat I have ever had, nor the most expensive one either. I couldn't bring myself to the thought of getting rid of it since it was my "salvation" covering me from the cold air every winter. The weight of it stayed close to me to keep out any drafts, like a warm heavy blanket on your bed at night. Everyone kept telling me I didn't need that heavy of a coat to wear to keep me warm but I didn't agree, till one year I tried a lighter coat and it did work just fine and I wasn't burdened by the weight of a heavy coat either.

You can tell the new Wisconsinites! They look like they're freezing because they don't want to wear heavy winter coats. They think they can bear the elements with what they choose to wear regardless of what is required or suggested to wear for protection. People do the same thing with spiritual warfare. They only want to wear what they choose, which is not really any protection at all against the enemy. Spiritually speaking; they are under-clothed, under-protected from satan's attacks.

Maybe you live in a warmer climate. You need sunscreen, appropriate clothing and hats to offer protection from the sun damaging your skin and the heat causing dehydration and exhaustion. On rainy days we wear rain boots, raincoats and use umbrellas. Why do we take such care to protect ourselves from the weather? To keep us from the elements that will ruin our clothes, hair, cause illness, etc.

When our soul isn't protected, it also becomes vulnerable to outside spiritual elements. The armor of God is one of the most important sets of garments we will ever wear. It can only be worn by believers, those who have been redeemed and are following Christ in a godly lifestyle after repentance. Armor is worn over our garments for protection from an enemy. It is the same for our spiritual bodies.

Why do we need the armor of God? Simple, when you joined God's eternal family you inherited His enemies also. Don't despair! You also **inherited God's power** and strength for fighting the enemies. Good thing huh? Yeah, all the power that God has is readily available for us if we choose to become a child of God and flee all manner of sin. You can't play both sides, there are no double agents in God's army.

The armor of God consists of garments that will equip the warrior for battle against the enemy. They include, but are not limited to, helmet of salvation, breastplate of righteousness, shield of faith, sword of the word of God, shoes of peace and the belt of truth. We will discuss each one in their own perspective chapters for more clarification.

As a teen I was not aware of spiritual things and left myself open to others' influence on me. We summoned up spiritual entities. I wanted to know if my dad ever loved me. So we called on my "dad", he had been dead for a few years. I asked questions of the "so called spirit" calling himself my dad and he said yes he did. We were just having fun, so we thought. One day we called on satan, don't ask me why, we just did. When the girl who was the medium spoke, her voice changed and through her a demon spoke and said that some of us believed in God and he said we were wrong for believing in God. When we told the demon to leave he said, "No." We couldn't make him leave. I remember praying and asking God to help us. Finally he left. I didn't know then but any small amount of faith in God can move an army of satanic forces. Real faith, not sit on the sidelines faith.

As most teens will attest, they are usually at odds with their parents. I was not immune to that either. One guy asked me if I wanted to put a curse on my mom or turn her into something. Since I didn't know anything about spiritual warfare I didn't realize I needed armor. I did read the word of God enough to know that he was offering me satanic power. I declined and then proceeded to tell him about the God I served and that the power he was offering was minimal. I hope I made an impact on him.

We definitely need armor at our workplace. I was working for a telemarketing firm. We were given partners to demonstrate how to get someone to change their mind and purchase something. The girl I had been partnered with knew I loved shoes. I assumed she would use that knowledge to get me to buy. However she didn't. She had told me she was part of a Wicca group. She knew I was a Christian. We had to do our demonstrations in front of the whole group. She asked me if I had wanted to have power to change others, put curses on them. She offered me power over other's lives. She tried to tell me why I should have it, what it could do for me. When my turn came to respond I told her, in front of the group, that I didn't need the power to change someone, God is the only one who can change anyone. She reminded me that there were people she and I didn't particularly like and maybe if we put curses on them they would suffer for their wrong doings. I said, "Why would I want to put a curse on someone? It would only make them madder and more sinful. It wouldn't change them at all. They are already unhappy. Why would I want to continue being mistreat by them? Why not ask God to bring salvation and healing *to them* so He can help them to change and become better, happier, godly people? Think about it. Then they would treat us better and all would be good." Hurt people hurt people. Healed people help others to heal. Wouldn't you rather be one who heals than one who hurts others?

There are many people who feel powerless. They dream of the day they will have power over someone or something. Then there are those who feel like they'll never have any power to change any part of their life. We shouldn't seek to control or have power over anyone. We should want relationships for the healthy benefits we bring to them and what we offer to others, in mutual respect and honoring them over ourselves, without becoming the doormat. I have always told my daughters to look for a mate who will help them to be the very best they can be. Someone who will put effort into the girl's lives, not just their own. We as women need to put into our mate's life also. Friendships are the same. We will always benefit from being a giver.

Let's look at each garment of warfare and how it reflects on us, our relationship to God and our relationships with others. Come join me on this special spiritual awareness. Opening our "closets" to better equip us for our journey through this life on our way to Heaven.

Journal page for chapter seventeen, Our Spiritual Wardrobe, the Armor of God

On this page I would like for you to write down all the ways in the past you have tried to protect yourself. What did you learn about our spiritual enemies in this chapter? Are there any other doors you may have opened of a spiritual nature in the past that you need to close?

What is Salvation, and why do I need it?

As I mentioned in the last chapter, you cannot wear the armor of God without being in His family. Adoption has its privileges. Remember Tamar was King David's daughter. She was royalty. Just as Tamar had the privilege to wear her royal garments, so we too have permission to wear the garments of *our royal godly family*. Anyone else who tried to wear royal robes were trying to usurp a position that was not theirs to take. Although our spiritual garments do not *appear* costly, they are indeed of the **highest** value. Christ paid the price, offering His life so we could have all we would ever need, even share in His spiritual garments.

To understand salvation, we need to back up to why we needed saving in the first place. In the beginning, Adam and Eve rejected God's warning, do not eat. Then, His people rejected God's laws, the 10 commandments, which were set up to guide them. Next, they rejected God's messengers, the prophets, who spoke words from God. Then they rejected God's only Son, Jesus Christ, who came to save us all from sin. Jesus said He would send them a helper, the Holy Spirit, they rejected the Holy Spirit also. When they did that, refused the *God-sent* Holy Spirit; they rejected the one who sent him. They have rejected everyone God sent, clearly still in a state of rebellion.

God did not create us to be separated from him. As a mother, I did not have children so someone else would raise them. I wanted to share my life with them, to love, nurture and teach them what I knew. I wanted to tell them about their creator God, and what He has done for me, to have a relationship with them. Parenthood is a **forever thing**. I will always be their mother, they will always be my children. It is that way with God too. You were meant to be His. He wants you in His life with Him in Heaven—forever.

Have you ever read the end of a story to find out how it ends? Does it ruin the book if you do? Well this one won't. The end, found in Revelation, is just the beginning. Yes, it is true! Our end of this world is just the beginning of our future, either in heaven or hell, depending on who we choose to follow and believe. We hold our futures in our own hands, or rather our hearts. Who does your heart belong to? Who will you serve for the remaining years, months, days of your life? Only one can fulfill any promises of a beautiful future with an outstanding amazing inheritance in heaven. The other one satan, as I mentioned before is an imitator. False teachers lead people astray, but if we don't read the Word of God for ourselves, we become liable for our own fate.

Satan was full of pride and wanted to be worshiped as God. God alone is to be worshipped and in His sovereign wisdom had to get rid of pride and sin. He sent satan down to the earth. God's enemy has a goal to destroy anything godly or good. Satan wants to have you follow his deceptive ways, lying to you, and saying you are free. The lie is that you are in more bondage than if you were under the care and design of God Almighty. Fun is short lived. *Joy is everlasting*.

We must first make a decision for salvation before we are fitted for the King's Royal Service. He chose us prior to salvation, or what I like to call adoption. After salvation **He renews us to our former family position** and *dresses us for* our *preplanned, perfectly designed destiny* to be fulfilled. Oh, and it is a marvelous thing to be in his divine plan for your life. Nothing in this world compares to being in your "element." (A place where you know you belong and are equipped to do the job, task with such efficiency that it comes natural and easily). It is God given, God equipped, God ordained, God sustained. Oh yeah. It doesn't get any better than that this side of heaven. His presence is evident and you are filled in such a way that peaceful resolve overflows.

God wants a relationship with you.

- Will you choose life from your Loving Creator God?
- Will you choose life from the Words of God, found in the Bible?
- Will you choose Jesus as your provision for freedom from the bondages of sin, and from the consequences of sin, which is eternity in hell?
- Will you choose to allow the finishing work on this earth by the God-given, God sent, Holy Spirit in your life?

The Bible says, "Now is the time for salvation, choose this day whom you will serve. You cannot serve two gods." One brings death, one has and always will bring life. What holds you back from choosing life with God? Who holds you back? Is it due to a hurt done to you from a church member, or someone leading you to follow them away from God? We allow those who have hurt us in the past to continue to do so, if we let them keep us from God and his healing. They'll keep you from God's blessings and your ultimate destiny, designed *specifically for you for this your time in history*.

This is about you and God alone. Won't you consider relinquishing your life and pain to a loving God? Will you today, choose to live your life under God's direction, thus fulfilling your original God-given destiny? Repentance is merely asking and receiving forgiveness and turning totally around in your life. Fleeing all sin and now serving God instead of your fleshly wants. No longer following anything that is not of God. Pursuing a life filled with God, your loving father.

It starts with:

- Admitting to God, you have sinned, which we all have done.
- Asking God for His forgiveness and accepting His forgiveness.
- Believing that Christ is the only way to God.
- Accepting Jesus' death and resurrection as payment for your past sins.

Here is a short prayer to follow:

Salvation Prayer:

Dear God, I confess that I am a sinner, I have sinned
against you and I am in need of your forgiveness. I
repent of my sins and willingly leave them behind. I
accept Jesus as my personal savior and Lord of my life.
Amen

After that, it is important for you to:

- Let go of all ties and/or relationships★ that keep you from God.
- Flee, turn from, all sinful harmful habits, accepting God's help in addictions.
- Renounce all ties with any and all satanic practices.

Now what?

Joy unspeakable . . . . the word of God says the angels in heaven rejoice over a new believer of God. You now have a reason to rejoice, you are free from sins bondage.

Full of glory . . . It is true, the Glory of God is revealed in His creation. You are now a new creation in Christ Jesus, filled with his likeness unto eternal Glory.

The rest of your life . . . It will become a new beginning for you as of today's salvation.

When you make this commitment, ***rejoice, we are now eternally sisters***! I will see you in heaven. We can have all sorts of great times together. Who knows, maybe I will meet you before then. That would be great. I love making new friends! I am so excited for you. I would love to just grab and hug you and say I love you and welcome you to the family! Your spiritual inheritance has just been activated!

For fun, there is a simple Adoption page at the end of the Appendix for you to fill in as a new family member to God's royal family tree.

★When I mention removing relationships that keep you from God, marriage is a bit different. God's word says we may win them to Christ by our godly actions.

But, if there is *any* abuse, you need to get help right away and if need be, leave the home till the abusive issues have been resolved. Many women have lost their lives at the hands of their abusers. Others have been deeply emotionally and physically harmed.

For a fuller description on why we needed saving see Appendix under <u>What is Salvation and why do I need it.</u>

Closet purging time for,
What is salvation, and why do I need it?

Here's another "add to your closet" item, a new journal. Keeping a journal for your new life in Christ is a great idea. I use mine as a prayer journal. A journal that I write my prayers to God, my needs, prayer concerns for other's needs. I date them and watch and see God meet those needs. My faith is encouraged by seeing Him work in those areas of my life.

Journal page for chapter eighteen,
What is Salvation, and why do I need it?

On this page I'd like you to consider *what you will do with* the knowledge of Christ's sacrifice for you and His offer of Salvation to you. Did you accept his offer? If not, what holds you back from accepting the adoption papers that will enable Him to welcome you into His family? What new things have you learned about Christ and the Father God in this Chapter?

Helmet of Salvation

We cover our heads for warmth from the cold, for shade from the hot sun. I love hats!! For me, a hat covers the lack of ability I have in hairstyles. I really am a poor hairdresser. On a plane recently an older gentleman said to me, "Look over there, you don't see that very often anymore." I asked him what he was referring to and he said, "The lady over there with the hat. Used to be you would see women wear hats in church all the time." He seem pleasantly surprised when I said that I agreed. Then I admitted I love hats too, and have been wearing them in church. In the past women used to wear veils in church as a covering. I remember wearing lace circles on my head in church as a child.

A warrior wears a helmet to protect his head from weapons of warfare that could damage their vision, hearing, brain or cause death. I crashed a moped trying to learn how to ride it and three days later I couldn't remember words or complete sentences. There were several times I had to pray my way home. I took turns I didn't mean to while driving and said things backwards for a while. I really could've used some head protection! I had a long journey of healing my brain from the injury. They said the brain was bruised and it would take time to heal like the rest of my bruises, which were the size of grapefruits. They took a year to heal. The doctors have diagnosed me as having short-term memory loss. They also said I had above average intelligence, great now where did I put it?

Spiritually the helmet is the part of the armor that protects our mind, thoughts and decisions. That includes our emotional state, our knowledge, learning ability in the brain, the decision-making part of us, and our life's vision from all enemies physical and spiritual. Our spiritual enemies include those that can keep us from God, those that pervert our minds towards ungodly thoughts, ideas and decisions. An enemy is one who will tempt you toward anything that can become an addiction, whether it is sex, porn, alcohol, smoking, drugs, overeating, under eating, etc. Jesus said in the New Testament:

Mark 7:20-23
"And he said, that which comes out of the man that defiles the man.
For from within, out of the heart of men, precede evil thoughts,
adulteries, fornications, murders, Thefts, covetousness, wickedness,
deceit, lasciviousness, an evil eye, blasphemy, pride, foolishness:
All these evil things come from within, and defile the man."

Physical enemies are those that can injure or kill the physical body, mind and soul. They also include drug or alcohol abuse and eating disorders. Workaholics who stress themselves out are also at risk of physical harm, running themselves into the ground to get ahead, they are relentless. I'm admittedly too distractible to do that. ***Anything that can distract us from our goals can become an enemy to our future.*** That's something I have to work on for sure. Watching too much television can be harmful too. You've heard the old saying, "Garbage in, garbage out." There is so much negativity in shows on television that we become negative and depressed, even fearful of impending harm. I love a good crime mystery, but after a few too many, I become more fearful of what could happen to me. We weren't meant to be able to handle all that negativity in our lives. It starts to affect our health. What or how much we watch does make a difference. We begin to feel inadequate about ourselves. Face it, not many people look like the models, but they have flaws too.

Don't think the values on television are good and honest or worthy of following. Much has been distorted on the news, showing only the media's view. Family viewing times now promote ungodly lifestyles. Satan uses our TVs, the music we listen to and the public opinion to get into our minds, promoting jealousy, envy, greed, vengeance, adultery, confusing gender issues, etc. Watching the food commercials makes us hungry for a burger or ice cream. The cable shows may have *something good*, but then *we don't live our own lives anymore. We become what we spend the most time with. We* live vicariously through what is on the television instead of getting ourselves into the real world and doing fun things on our own.

So instead of being a couch potato, get involved somewhere, learn something new, try a new class, make new friends and take a walk. Visit some old friends, they're probably missing you too. We may be afraid of relationships, but if we don't make friends and be a part of something other than ourselves, we become lonely and irritable and self-serving and maybe self-righteous too. No one on their deathbed wishes they had more money. We want to know we were loved, that we will be missed and made a difference for good in someone's life. We can't do that if we don't participate in anyone's life.

Emotional trauma is another issue. If you are reading this book for your own healing, you know what emotional trauma is. Post-traumatic stress disorder is very real for abuse survivors. Please don't minimize or underestimate the emotional pain, trauma that you have experienced. It actually hinders your healing process by ignoring it. Trust me, those around you already know that you have issues. It boils over in your actions, choice of words, attitudes in an argument. Anger will come out, and it has to, but to what degree is up to you. Hiding pain never works, it always finds an outlet. Unfortunately some become addicts to numb the pain. Denial may be part of the healing process but you can't stay there.

As I mentioned before, I recommend you go to a counselor for your emotional trauma. They will also offer you PTSD counseling. I prefer a Christian counselor, one who will direct you towards the ONE true Healer, God the Father. It is true you may need to go to a few counselors before you find the right one for you. Don't give up.

I had to overcome a lot myself in my process of healing. I used to talk about it a lot, but no one would help me through it. All I wanted was someone to walk the journey of healing with me. Holding me, crying with me, supporting me in prayer and directing me to the Word and the Lord. You don't think straight when you are in pain. Feeling alone makes you feel more vulnerable too, like you can't trust anyone. The word of God and the work of the

Holy Spirit's counseling has helped me through a lot of my emotional issues. God's word stands true. Give your tears to God and your pain, tell Him how you feel and let him be your healer. No one can do it like HIM, no one. That is another reason I am writing this book, I don't want you to feel alone in your journey of healing. Thanks for joining me on mine. It is comforting knowing I am not alone.

Tamar *couldn't* return to her Royal destiny. She missed out on so much in her life. Don't let your emotional trauma keep you desolate. Rise above it. Pull up all your courage and do the hard work to overcome and get your confidence back. You are so valuable. You do have great strength and with God's help you can and will overcome the effects of the trauma. Time heals. You may not forget, but it won't have the same hold over you that it once did.

All of us do have some sort of trauma in our lives. Who hasn't been picked on in school for one reason or another? Some may have injuries to their bodies that trigger emotional issues too. Used to be if you had lost a leg, or arm you were treated unfairly, left out, treated with shame. Now we make films based on the struggles and successes of those who have overcome their obstacles and prevailed. Not only do they succeed, they are the greatest encouragers I know. We love to root for the underdogs. When the underlings get the big jobs, we do a little victory dance, Oh Yeah!

That's what I want for you.

To succeed to the point of not only healing your heart and mind, but putting you back in the seat of your own God given destiny. Believe it, **God is not done with you yet.** He has so much in store for you.

Jeremiah 29:11
"For I know the thoughts that I think toward you,
saith the LORD, thoughts of peace, and not of evil,
to give you an expected end."

2Timothy 1:7
"For God hath not given us the spirit of fear;
but of power, and of love, and of a sound mind."

Revelations 21:4
"And God shall ***wipe away all tears*** from their eyes
and there shall be no more death, neither sorrow, nor crying, neither
shall there be any more pain: for the former things are passed away."

Isaiah 26:3
"He will keep anyone in perfect peace,
when their mind *is* stayed *on HIM:*
because they trust in HIM."

We only have one mind. We can only be deceived by our mind. Our hearts and thoughts trigger our mind, which triggers our decision-making. We don't want to look stupid, so we join the group. We don't want to look or feel poor so we beg, borrow or steal to attain what we think we need to have to be a part of the norm. We push away anyone who stands for something that may make us feel bad if we don't believe the same way. That is why I believe the helmet of salvation is so important. Protect the head at all costs. **That is all satan has to work with**. He can't physically make us do anything. He uses our hearts, sorrows, pain, anger and hurts to get us to think his way and rebel from our heavenly father God. Satan uses the truth of our own pain to trick us into believing half-truths about the situation we face. We put our focus on the other person with hate and vengeance, we are easily agitated, but blame everyone else for our bad behaviors. Some delve more into their addictions and then satan uses guilt to get them into other negative behaviors.

The old bait and switch. He tempts us, keeps us in the addictions by lying to us telling us we need them, we can't live without them, we deserve them, they'll make us happy, when in fact they weaken us to further addictions and harm. We no longer have any freedom, addictions RULE you, not the other way around. You can't control them. Satan reminds us of our shame and guilt, even after he was the one to tempt us, then he shoves it in our faces to further injure us. He just loves making us look bad. He is known as the deceiver, Lucifer, the devil, satan, slave owner. People become slaves to their addictions. **But I thank my God that there is a way out from all of them**. One-step at a time. First salvation, then clean up. **God doesn't expect you to get clean before He accepts you.** He *accepts you,* cleans up your wounds, heals the pain and gives you strength over addictions, the things that have enslaved you. **Slaves can't free themselves.** You were bought with a price, Christ's shed blood. It's up to you to accept that as payment for your freedom. It won't matter how you got there, He is ready and willing to get you out of it. The one who created your body knows what you need to get through the process of healing those addictions. Plan on having accountability for your healing process. Don't do it alone, let someone help you through it. There are many churches and places that can help you detoxify. Like I mentioned before, Focus on the Family will help anyway they can. Don't let the shame of where you have come from keep you from your future. Press on to new heights, new strengths.

Know the truth and the truth will set you free. God's word is truth.

John 14:6
"Jesus saith unto him,
I am the way, the truth, and the life:
no man cometh unto the Father, but by me."

With our minds we seek God's truth or run from it. With our minds we make decisions to either live according to God's word, or decide to believe in Christ as our Savior or choose to follow satan and the world's ways. Satan is in charge of the world until Christ comes again to receive those who are HIS. We also make good or bad choices based on our previous belief systems. There are a few scriptures warnings I'd like to share with you.

Proverbs 30:12
"*There is* a generation *that are* pure *in their own eyes,*
and *yet* are not washed from their filthiness."

Isaiah 5:21
"Woe unto *them that are* wise *in their own eyes,*
and prudent in their own sight!"

Titus 1:15
"Unto the pure all things *are* pure: but unto them that are defiled and unbelieving
is nothing pure; but even their mind and conscience is defiled."

Using *our own* judgment or experiences to tell us what is good or bad, acceptable or not acceptable is not a good idea. Here's the problem: we may have been taught wrong by our family experiences. That is why so many abused become abusers. That is normal to them. Acceptable. But it isn't acceptable, nor should it be normal for anyone. If we can't use our own judgment, what **can** we use to decide what is good or bad? The Bible was written for our learning by our Creator God. The helmet of Salvation protects us from our own thoughts **by lining them up with and directing them to God and His words, the Bible.** You only need to look up www.e-sword.com online, simply choose a word and it will bring up scriptures showing how to deal with the issues that you are facing.

In the Old Testament, King Solomon was the wisest man in his time. When King David was going to crown his son, he gave this speech in 1 Chronicles basically at Solomon's inauguration ceremony. He had a position to fulfill, like you have a divine position to fulfill. No one else can do yours. Therefore, **if we don't accomplish our own predetermined God given destiny, something in history will be missing.**

I hope as you read this you will know it is meant for all who have a royal destiny, which is all of us, namely YOU.

1Chronicles 28:8, 9
"Now therefore in the sight of all Israel the congregation of the LORD,
and in the audience of our God, **keep and seek for all the commandments
of the LORD your God**: that ye may possess this good land,
and leave *it* for an inheritance for your children after you forever.
And thou, Solomon my son, know thou the God of thy father, and serve him
with a perfect heart and with a willing mind: for the LORD searches all hearts,
and understand all the imaginations of the thoughts: **if thou seek him, he
will be found of thee;** but if thou *forsake him, he will cast thee off forever.*"

Your footprint in this world, makes a better impression when you are walking upright.

Upright in mind, body and spirit. It is my prayer that you seek Him, while he may be found. That you leave a godly heritage. You can't afford to waste anymore of your precious years on the negative painful past. It keeps you from experiencing your exciting future.

After all, we girls like to have fun, right? Real fun is enjoying yourself free from addictions and harm. It's when you and your friends leave happier and blessed because you were together and not offended by each other, encouraged but not ripped apart. We can be supported through life's journeys in ways that benefit, not destroy our mind or health or spiritual walk towards heaven. It is my hope that I am able to support you in some small way on this your journey through the Word of God towards your healing.

If you have become a new believer, congrats! You are on your way to a new you. You may not recognize the new you, but will learn to love being her. Don't be fearful of becoming someone you won't like. You will be the best you've ever imagined, except of course, by God. He has imagined good things for you all along, just waiting for you to come to Him. If you haven't made a decision of where you stand with God yet, journal that and all your feelings, fears, challenges, doubts, anger, everything. God knows it all anyway, you won't surprise him in anyway.

Genesis 16:13
"Thou art a God that sees me."
Psalms 139:17
"How precious also are your thoughts towards me, O God."

You are loved regardless of your choice here. Jesus chose the cross because of the love He has for us; so we wouldn't be separated from God.

John 3:16–18
"For God so loved the world, that he gave his only begotten Son,
that whosoever believeth in him should not perish, but have everlasting life.
For God sent not his Son into the world to condemn the world; but that
the world through him might be saved. He that believeth on him is not
condemned: but he that believeth not is condemned already, because
he hath not believed in the name of the only begotten Son of God."

The expected end for all believers of Jesus Christ and His Father God are eternity in Heaven with God, Jesus, the Holy Spirit and all those who have gone before us and will follow us there. Jesus' words encourage us to follow Him back to God.

Want to know for sure if you are going to heaven? ★ First read Romans. Then read John chapters 1-3. If you are curious about how this story ends read the last book Revelations. The Bible will come true, all of it. So now is a good time to open it up and see for yourself what's in store for you. There will be a new heaven and earth, and a place for YOU!

★See Appendix under Helmet of Salvation for more information on Salvation.

Closet purging time for,
Helmet of Salvation

You may store your DVDs or CDs somewhere other than your closet, but I'd like you to go through them and see if what you have goes against the Word of God. Not just anti-Christian, but anything that hinders your spiritual growth. Any books that don't reflect the purity of a wholesome life you may want to get rid of. What goes into the mind will eventually come out somewhere in our thoughts, mind, words we speak. So do inventory and prayerfully consider purging those from your house. I remember as a new believer I had gone through my music collection and went to the dump and shot them up with a 22 rifle. It was great fun and I have to admit it was freeing to let go of the negative influence that it had in my life.

Journal page for chapter nineteen, Helmet of Salvation

Our minds need to be protected from lies. The temptations of the flesh that are never satisfied. On this page, write down what you thought about my asking you to get rid of your unhealthy books, DVDs and CDs. What did you learn about how we need to protect our mind? What will you change in your life to add to your knowledge? What new thing will you learn to enjoy? Did you choose salvation? Why or why not?

Baptism Garment

After shedding all of the bad, unwanted, unworthy garments, it is nearly time to put on the wonderful new **Spiritual wedding garments** of God's design. However, before you put on the new garments, baptism of the heart and soul is a great thing to do next. Why baptism? When we are dirty from our daily activities, we shower or bathe to remove the dirt and sweat from our fleshly bodies. We feel clean and refreshed and awakened. Similarly, we need to be cleansed from our stained past.

In the Bible, it was customary for the host of a home to wash the guest's feet upon their arrival, it was a sign of hospitality. Their journey was dusty and this act kept their home from getting contaminated with the dirt from the outside. I don't know about you, but scrubbing floors is not my favorite thing to do. Similarly, we don't want to bring in anything from our past into the new life with Christ. We need a spiritual washing of mind, body and soul. No one puts on a wedding garment without first bathing.

Scripturally, baptism follows salvation. It represents God cleansing us of our old selves and frees us up for the new to come and flow over us. It is a letting go of the past and freeing our hearts and minds for the new future self. **Spiritually**, it also opens the door to a closer walk with God. Baptism is an acceptance of cleansing that God has done for us, in us and through us.

If you, *like me,* were baptized as an infant by the conviction of your parents, please understand that infant baptism is not found in the scriptures. Infant baptism is a *tradition* in some churches. The Word of God specifically says to first, believe on the Lord Jesus Christ, then repent, ask God for forgiveness, accept Christ as your Savior and then be baptized. An infant hasn't committed any sins. Since there is nothing to repent of, there is no need for baptizing. They don't know who Jesus is, therefore God protects the children. Infant baptism won't keep you from sin, nor will it keep an adult safe from hell. If it could, there wouldn't be a lot of sinners, since many parents baptize infants, hoping it will save their children's souls. There also would be no need for penance and confessions with priests when we are older, if infant baptism was a means of keeping us from sin. But we all know that we have sinned. Baptism is what you do for yourself, as an adult, when you have made a decision for your own beliefs and dedication to God.

1 John 2:12
"I write unto you, little children,
because your sins are forgiven you for his name's sake."

1 John 2:1
"My little children, these things I write unto you, that ye sin not. And if *any* **man**
sin, we have an advocate with the Father, Jesus Christ the righteous."

Parents now choose to have a baby dedicated. Dedication of a child is a parent asking God to bless their children and help the parents to raise those children up for His Glory. You can do this at any time in their young lives, not just at birth. It is the parent's role to live out their faith, then teach that to their children. It is helpful to attend church with your children, you can learn together. The age of reasoning is around eight years old. That is why it is so important to teach the children about the Bible and Jesus while they are young. I taught my daughters about baptism when they were eight years old. We spent six months working through the Word of God learning why we should be baptized and how it is done. Now, my husband and I are pleased to know our daughters are reading the Word of God and training their children about God and Jesus. It is so reassuring to know they are following what they were taught.

I decided to have a rebaptism for myself a few years ago. I wanted the chance to make a defined moment where I pushed past my painful memories. A moment where God washed away all the lies and fears I believed about myself and the doubts about God really wanting me in his family. It was my time to accept that I was a daughter of *"The King."* I chose to release my fears of failure and accept myself for who I was created to be. I had to trust God to do the healing, for cleansing all my past. It wasn't easy, since trust is a major issue with me. I had to take a moment to let go of fear and just let the pastor proceed. I came up with a renewed sense of belonging to someone, namely God.

Baptism is what you do for yourself as an adult for your own beliefs and dedication to God. How do you know if you are ready for baptism? I always tell others to pray first, read the Word of God on baptism and then talk with your pastor about proceeding with the plans.

Baptism of the Holy Spirit

Whether or not your church experience has taught you anything about the Baptism of the Holy Spirit, it is indeed part of the whole Word of God, the Bible. It is found in the New Testament, which is where we get our basic training for how to live the new Christian life. The first believers, the disciples, were told by Jesus himself that when he went to the Father he would send the Holy Spirit. God sent Jesus; we need to accept Jesus for our salvation. Jesus sent the Holy Spirit for us **as a guide, counselor and comforter.** He was sent to help us on the rest of our journey towards heaven. Some people receive the Holy Spirit upon water baptism, some seek him later on.

Luke 3:16
"John answered, saying unto *them* all, I indeed baptize you with water;
but one mightier than I cometh, the latchet of whose shoes I am not worthy
to unloose: he shall baptize you with the Holy Ghost and with fire."

It is scriptural to receive and be full of the Holy Spirit.

Acts 19:1-6
"Paul having passed through the upper coasts came to Ephesus:
and finding certain disciples, He said unto them, Have ye received
the Holy Ghost since ye believed? And they said unto him,
"We have not so much as heard whether there be any Holy Ghost".
And he said unto them, "Unto what then were ye baptized?"
And they said, Unto John's baptism. Then said Paul, John verily
baptized with the baptism of repentance, saying unto the people,
that they should believe on him, which should come after him, that is,
on Christ Jesus. When they heard *this,* they were baptized in the
name of the Lord Jesus. And when Paul had laid *his* hands upon them,
the Holy Ghost came on them; and they spoke with tongues, and prophesied."

Luke 4:1
"And Jesus being full of the Holy Ghost
returned from Jordan, and was led
by the Spirit into the wilderness."

Micah 3:8
"But truly I am full of power
by the spirit of the LORD."

Deuteronomy 34:9
"And Joshua the son of Nun was
full of the spirit of wisdom;
for Moses had laid his hands upon him."

I know there are people who are afraid of who, or what the Holy Spirit is. He is **part of God,** sent by Jesus, to be for us, not against us. He is **holy**. He is **on a mission to assist us in every area of our lives.** He should know how to get us to where we are going, since he came from Heaven. Do not fear Him or the words or directions He gives you. They are directly from God. Trust God to use the Holy Spirit to complete you. (Note, follow directions that are consistent with the Bible, not harmful demonic voices.)

As you heed His warnings and directives, you will find yourself fulfilled. You will be surprised and thankful to God that you had the Holy Spirits leading. I found there are a lot of misconceptions about how to receive the gifts of the Holy Spirit. I had heard rumors that people who spoke in tongues were crazy and weird, hanging from the chandeliers and running down aisles of churches. Not exactly what I would want to be doing to honor my Lord. Nowhere in the Bible does it say that after you have the Holy Spirit you will do such things.

When I am around those who use their prayer language, as it is sometimes called, I feel nearer the throne of God. I get a sense of God's presence and often I have tears of emotion and afterwards peace. You don't have to have the prayer language to be saved. However, you won't have the benefit of the strength it gives you, nor the direct line of assistance from the Holy Spirit to reach the throne of God.

I have found the Holy Spirit to be of great benefit in my life. He has been through it all *with* me. He has *kept me from the presence* of evil. He has shown me *a way of escape* from sin when I was tempted. He has *directed me* in several paths and shown me who to help. He has *given me words to say* to comfort and help on their journey. Most recently he has *given me the courage* to write these words for you. It is my prayer that you seek the wisdom of God in this area of your life as well.

Closet purging time for, Baptism Garment

I always like to think outside the box, or in this case closet. Consider having a makeover done by your favorite salon, or a friend. Do a whole head to toe makeover, hairstyle, and maybe hair color, make up and clothing. Maybe now is a good time to do a little garment window shopping. Try on new styles that you would normally never try and see what it does for your figure and your sense of a whole new YOU. Make sure to do before and after pictures. Make it more fun and have a makeover party with your friends.

Redoing your closet is like baptism, a whole new you! Have fun as you empty the old and fill it with new garments that are truly a reflection of the real you.

Journal page for chapter twenty,
Baptism Garment

Use this page to describe your view on baptism before and after reading this chapter. Write down what it would mean to you to have a new spiritual wedding garment, the garment of baptism. Have you been baptized since childhood? What steps will you take to become baptized in a church? What have you learned about the spiritual baptism of the Holy Spirit? List any fears you have about being filled with the Holy Spirit as the scriptures declare. What strengths will you have after you receive the gifts of the Holy Spirit?

Sword of the Word of God
(The Bible)

The Word of God, the Bible, is the part of the Armor of God that is the **Sword**. The sword is a weapon of **offense,** not defense. In other words, you would **use it to strike the enemy before he strikes you**.

Hebrews 4:12
"For the word of God *is* quick, and powerful,
and sharper than any two-edged sword, piercing even to the
dividing asunder of soul and spirit, and of the joints and marrow,
and *is a discerner of the thoughts and intents of the heart.*"

You would need to know the words of God to be able to use that weapon properly. You must have a real knowledge of the word to master and maneuver this weapon with ease and precision. Knowing the word of God also gives insight into the mind of our enemy satan. It gives us clear instructions as to how we can defeat satan, and thwart his plans to destroy us.

Why do I bring up the Word of God, the Bible all the time? If it weren't for God in my life I wouldn't be who I am today, nor would I have had the victories I experienced in my life. For me, and many of you, God *is the reason* we are still sane and alive. I cannot think of any greater help to give you than the words of my Lord and Savior Jesus Christ and my Father God, the Creator of all things.

The Word of God is for teaching and lovingly sharing Godly truths for living in this world. It is for healing, health, wisdom, a greater vision, exhortation and encouragement. When we read it, we will get to **know and understand our Creator, through His letters** and the plans He has for us—a future with HIM. Freedom from sin and all bondages.

When you read a book and you enjoy it, you will find yourself recommending it to others. You know they will share the same or similar benefit from the book. If the book is part of a series, you begin to see a pattern to the author's writing style. You look forward to the next chapter, the next book in the series. We all hate it when we are left with the cliffhangers. Later, you may read an autobiography of the author. You begin to correlate the books they wrote to the author's life and thoughts. You could say you might even feel like you know them, in part. So, work with me here. When you read the word of God, realize it is just that, the Words of God. You will begin to learn **who** He is, **what** He thinks, **how** He reacts, **that** He Loves much, He **has** judgments, He **still** forgives, and a lot more. When you read His words in the Bible you begin to *know HIM*, simple as that.

The books in the Bible include men and women's lives being changed by the works of Christ and the Holy Spirit. We read accounts of Him in their lives, or in some cases those who didn't choose Him. You may not like that God's Word has consequences. You might ask, "Why must I have judgments? If God is love, why can't he just forgive everyone for everything?" When you are offended do you not want an apology? When someone is murdered do we not all cry out for justice? When we lose our jobs we want compensation. There is justice for all, but not always in all things. God is justified in His actions, choosing to defend His honor, His children and His Word. His word is true and holy. **It's prophesies will all be completed,** the good and the bad.

I recently watched a show where celebrities were asked if stranded on a deserted island what book would they bring. Not one mentioned a Bible, but then I didn't think they would. One person said they wanted a book that would be enjoyable no matter how many times they read it. A book that would bring meaningful words over and over again. So, I began to think how it pertains to this chapter. Would *you* want a Bible with you on a deserted island? For me, the more I read the Bible, the more I get out of it. I can read a passage one day, read the same thing a different day and each time it has a new meaning or revelation in it. Depending on my life's circumstances, it brings me many things, such as peace in my storms, direction in the fog of life's decisions and turmoil, comfort in loneliness, healing for my soul. It brings correction where I need it, (always done by conviction, not condemnation), hope when all seems lost, strength to continue, and so much more. It will never grow old because it is a *Living Word of* GOD. That means *it is alive and working through the pages to whoever will read it.*

If that isn't enough reason to get you started reading the word of God, maybe this will. If a manual were written to a parent to help raise a child, would you benefit from that? If a manual were written for newlyweds, would you offer it to them? If a manual were written for getting through the struggles in this life, (and we all have them!) would you read it? If a manual was written to give us instructions for healthy living, would you go out to buy it? Well, there is one, for all that and more, in the Word of God. Yes, really. No kidding here. Old and New Testaments have all that and more in them. The accounts of the mistakes and victories of people's lives. All written out for us to use as a reference and a guide towards a better life here on earth. We don't have to wait till we get to Heaven to enjoy our lives. He offers so much in the words He left for us.

Revelations 21:4
"And God shall **wipe away all tears** from their eyes;
and there shall be no more death, neither sorrow, nor crying, neither
shall there be any more pain: for the former things are passed away."

Doesn't that scripture above sound wonderful? Full of peace and hope and rest? Wouldn't you like to be able to have all that? It is yours for the taking. Adoption papers are all ready for you. You have already been chosen, will you accept the Father as yours? I hope you enjoy the benefits of reading the words of our Lord. The Word of God references us and Jesus Christ as Bride and Groom. He's the Groom, we the church, are His Bride.

Don't take *my* word for it, search it out for yourself. After all, it's *your life* we are talking about. You need to find God for yourself. It is the sole decision of each one of us to determine our life's direction and final destiny through Christ. Although it is strongly urged that you read and follow the words of our Creator.

Revelations 1:3
"Blessed is he that reads,
and they that hear the words of this prophecy,
and keep those things, which are written therein:
for the time *is* at hand."

Closet purging time for,
Sword of the Word of God

Nothing to purge from this chapter, however I am recommending a book to you. It is one that will enrich your life, change your perspective on your circumstances, reveal secrets, give you strength in weak areas and reveal a secret love that has been there for you since well, forever. Will you join me in reading the most wonderful book called the Bible? I myself am not easily prone to memorization. I have read the entire Bible several times and, like the movies we all enjoy, after seeing them a few times we begin remembering them. Reading the Word of God is like that. The more we read it the more we will remember about it. Try out the different versions of the Bible, see which one is easier for you to read, then add it to your daily life.

Today there are so many options for opening up our minds and hearts to the word of God, phone Apps, online, DVD's, CD's. They're all encouraging us to get familiar with the mind and heart of our creator God. That's what the book is all about. HIM and US.

Journal page for chapter twenty-one,
Sword of the Word of God

In this section of journaling I'd like you to write down any misconceptions you have had about reading the Word of God the Bible. What has kept you from reading it? What have you learned in this chapter that will help you understand the importance of reading the words God left for us? What steps will you take to use the words for you benefit? Memorization takes time but is well worth the effort.

Breastplate of Righteousness

Previously we talked about how the helmet protects the mind. The breastplate, which is also part of the armor of God, is worn over the shoulders and covers all the vital organs. When you consider the loss of any one of those, you begin to see how important it is to have the breastplate in place during battle, protecting you from enemy attacks. How does it protect us from the enemy? When you are living righteously, you are under the protection of God. He becomes that breastplate around you like body armor. He surrounds you with His protective love and wisdom, direction and peace. It is not heavy to wear, since God carries all the weight of our sin and sorrows. His yolk is easy and His burden light.

Protect your heart with the righteousness of God. Righteousness is an elusive thing if you are trying to do it all on your own. We don't have any righteousness of our own. Our fleshly selves are prone to evil and selfishness. That is why we need the filling of the Holy Spirit to become righteous. Spiritually, if you don't protect your heart, it will become darkened, and your final destination will not be very comfortable. If your heart is protected and good, being filled with God's spirit, your final destination is heaven.

Job 29:14a
"I put on righteousness, and it clothed me."

It is my privilege to offer you a hope and tell you He has a place prepared for you in His mansion. Do you want to be an overcomer? I do. It is freeing to be in the will of God, not bondage. When you make righteousness a priority, you won't have to worry about remembering what you say, because it will all be truth, no covering up what you are trying to hide. When righteousness is part of your wardrobe, you will feel fresh and honest and pure. Sin has a way of making us feel cruddy and heavy and overwhelmed, drained of mental and physical strength. We can ask the Father for what we need, according to His will and plan for our lives. If you find yourself in a state of unrighteousness, all you need to do is ask God for forgiveness and repent, that means turn around and sin no more. Not, ask forgiveness and return to the sin. You must leave it behind and take on righteousness as part of your wardrobe, your lifestyle from now on. He promises to forgive all who ask humbly. Most people feel freedom at that point of seeking God's forgiveness.

Righteousness is doing the right thing for the right reasons. Being in right standing with God. There are no "little sins." Sin is just that, sin. It may look like someone can get away with doing something wrong, but we shouldn't want to do that. We need to live as close to God's Word as we can, not live as close to the world as we can and still call ourselves a Christian. That's walking a fine line, behaving more like a disobedient child.

You may experience temptations to return to sinful behaviors, but don't do it. Be strong and overcome the enemy of our souls. Satan is the ultimate liar. He will tell you all manner of things to get you back on his side. Be prepared and read the Word of God, which is a living word, to keep your heart and mind on Him and His kingdom. Oh, I do so want to be in heaven with you as my sister. Stand firm and keep the faith, loving others as He has loved you. Take on the garment of righteousness and experience freedom.

Closet purging time for, Breastplate of Righteousness

I'd like for you to go through your closet and look for anything, it doesn't have to be clothing, which has been part of your past unrighteousness. Are there things that reminds you of past sins? Anything that brings a temptation back into a sinful lifestyle. Maybe some phone numbers need to be removed from your phone too? Remember it may feel painful to separate yourself from something you were attached to so long, but it will get easier and more freeing as you do.

Journal page for chapter twenty-two, Breastplate of Righteousness

Journal all the past sins that you feel you need to ask God for forgiveness. It's ok to use another piece of paper for this part. List as many as you can. No sin is too small, sin is sin. So mention it all to God. He already knows it, but he wants you to acknowledge it before Him. Ask Him to forgive each thing individually, not lump sum. Why? Because then you get the chance to realize each thing means something to God and to you in your process. We all have offended Him in many areas of our lives, including the sins of our words towards others. When you are done, journal how your prayer with God went. How did you feel after you asked for forgiveness? How was it to remove all from your heart? Are you experiencing more sleep, more energy yet? Keep on, you will.

Lingerie

I really want to talk about our sexuality in a way that is non-offensive and hopefully acceptable to most women, who want to love God and their current or future spouses. The clothes we wear reflect our moods and our perceived value of ourselves and what we perceive *others* want to see in us. We overdress, we underdress and yet we need to find balance and beauty in it all. Our sexuality is a gift from God. It is a blessing from God to give and receive pleasure with our spouse. The lingerie in our wardrobes reflect who we are sexually, morally, and what we hunger for in our hearts, bodies and minds. It can enhance your appearance by wearing sexy clothes and make you feel sensual and flirty. However, if after you have been abused, you feel the least bit dirty wearing sexy lingerie, don't choose it.

I don't recommend wearing anything that brings back past pain or gives you insecure feelings. After all, the moment is for the two of you, not to bring in anything from your past experiences. Many men like lingerie, but sexual intimacy has to do with an ongoing healthy relationship first, then we respond in the bedroom. Studies have proven women respond to loving, giving, tender relationships before they even get into bed with someone. Personally, I want to be loved, not sexed. Check out different styles of lingerie. Look for something that makes **you** feel feminine versus overtly sexy. Get comfortable with who YOU are first. Talk about the sexual part of the relationship in conversations before the actual act. Know what each of you prefers and make sure you both listen to each other's feelings and desires. No need to go out of your comfort zone to enjoy intimacy. Start slow and be there for each other. This is a love relationship. Love grows stronger as we bond together through each area of our lives. Pray through emotional times and let God heal your fears and insecurities. Does prayer for sex sound funny to you? It works. Everything God created was good and for our good. Others have made it sinful and exchanged intimacy for the lust of sex. When you start to feel sexed instead of loved, communicate that. My wish for you married women is that you come out of hiding from your sexuality and embrace your body as God made you a sexual being.

After I was married, I had to learn to allow myself to even accept pleasure because of the abuse I got as a small child. It was dirty to me and wrong. No PDA, public display of affection, for me! Dark room and no lights. I was afraid to dress sexy or flirty because I had incidents where I wasn't even dressed nice and men tried picking me up. Oh yeah the one-liners too. "I suppose if I play my cards right", "Can I buy you a drink?" As a tween I was forced on older men's laps and being laughed at when someone said I'd be "keeping them warm." I didn't want that kind of attention from abusers and perverts. I had enough of that growing up. I always felt shame being a female. Like I was dirty just being. I was not comfortable in my own skin, nor was I comfortable with my own sexuality.

One night I had a dream. I was in church and all of a sudden I realized I was naked. Yes, and in church no less. A woman brought me a blanket to cover myself with. God told me I shouldn't be ashamed of my body or my nakedness. It was not my sin. The sin belongs to those who had sinful, sexual thoughts about me. The shame belonged to them, not me. I had done no wrong. Good thing it was only a dream. I had taken the shame after the abuse. It wasn't mine to wear. It was theirs. But I kept putting it on since I was the one **shamed.** It took that dream to show me I was wearing **shame as a garment.**

Our bodies were not created to become toys. To give and receive pleasure, yes, in the context of marriage. We are to first build on the relationship as a foundation, so that when we get together for sexual intimacy and pleasure, it is for wholeness and oneness. A woman should feel **more** womanly and secure and loved in the act of sexual intimacy, not less. **God** gave women the ability to enjoy sexual intimacy.

I grew up thinking that if I didn't look like Barbie, I wasn't worth anyone taking a second glance. What girl didn't want to dress up like Barbie? All those beautiful gowns and accessories! Teens today experience so much more pressure to have sex sooner. They dream of becoming sexy and have desires to feel special and in love and become sensual. No one remains a teenager or young adult forever. But the actions we take from there affect us the rest of our lives. Somehow, we think that sexuality begins at puberty. Teens are not emotionally ready to handle or to sustain a relationship that is meant for marriage and having a family.

We need to encourage our teens and young women to wait for marriage for a sexual relationship. It is much more fulfilling. I'd rather trust a guy who waited for marriage than one who slept around. I'd be afraid he would leave me for someone else when he tired of me or something didn't go right, or worse yet leave me with diseases and emotional baggage. There is no commitment outside of marriage, no matter what a guy **says.** Women were made for companionship, not for having our bodies exploited. Women are deeply hurt after being dumped because we were made to have a mate for life, not a short-term relationship.

It is worth it to wait on God to find our mate. Notice, I didn't say perfect mate. There is no "perfect" anyone this side of heaven. We need to find a mate that will help complete us and be an encourager and supporter both financially and emotionally. One who will help us to become all we were meant to be and to follow God's **design** for our life. No little girl looks to her future and sees herself with a loser, working three jobs to support herself, her children and a lazy jobless boyfriend. She sees herself with Prince Charming, a beautiful wedding and a happily ever after.

So, where did we leave that behind and give up our dream guy, our wedding day and our financial security? If you can't find a decent guy, pray for God to deliver him to your door. Pray for him before God even reveals him to you. Keep looking, we deserve our Prince Charming.

Today's single woman can be honoring to God by how she dresses. The choices in our clothing really reflects our relationship to God and morality. Not every female had a good role model, so we all need to encourage each other to become the best we can be, no matter where we started out from. We *are* beautiful and if we can become confident, it will show in our appearance and attitudes about ourselves.

Then, there is the matter of experimenting with same sex relationships. God's Word is clear on that one. "He made man and woman and they became one," (Genesis 2:24). I would be remiss if I didn't tell you that God, our creator, also has a warning to those who stray from pure sexuality.

In 1 Corinthians 6:9 it says
"Do you not know that the unrighteous will not inherit the kingdom of God?
Do not be deceived. Neither fornicators, idolaters, adulterers,
homosexuals, sodomites, thieves, covetous, drunkards,
Revilers, nor extortionists, will inherit the kingdom of God.
And such were some of you.
But you were *washed,* you were *sanctified,* you were
justified in the name of the Lord Jesus and by the Spirit of our God."

Fornication—that means sex before marriage; lewd behavior—that means we should not have any overtly sexual vocabulary, provocative teasing or dressing like prostitutes.

A*dultery*—that means for any single person with a married person, or any two persons not married to each other but married to other mates.

Idolaters—are those who put anything above God, including themselves and their desires, worshiping idols made by man.

If you know anything about me, you'll know that I say this in love. I don't want you to have a life of death, but a life here *and* in heaven, which is why I share this with you. There has always been sin and temptations from the evil one, satan. Deception is his game, manipulating and putting thoughts into the heads of people is his torturous twisted method of trying to destroy what God loves. YOU. You are so valuable to God that satan can't stand you being whole and good and lovely. He used to be the most beautiful angel before God, but he wanted more. Pride became ugliness in him and God sent him out of heaven and onto the earth. God didn't design anyone for immorality nor homosexuality. It is our own desires and lusts and *misunderstanding of the temptations* of the enemy that takes us down those roads.

I know God has a plan for all of us even though we have been through many ugly things in our lives. It is my understanding that up to 50% of women who choose the lesbian lifestyle, do so *because* they were abused so badly from men. If that is you I am so sorry that you were treated in such a way as to leave your natural desires and needs of a man. Trust and healing are difficult in those situations. Please do know that not all men are sinful takers.

A while back I asked God to show me how it is that women get themselves into same sex relationships. I just didn't understand. Being a heterosexual and mainly protected from knowing anyone growing up that was gay or homosexual, I just didn't see what the draw was for a female to be interested in another female. Sure they joke around and say that what a woman really wants is "another woman". What they are really saying is that the women want their men to treat them with respect and love and nurture them. Which is something women do freely. But this is a serious thing, especially in the church setting. So I asked God to help me to understand this whole phenomenon.

Be careful what you pray for. As the days went on, I had this strange voice tell me, "Go kiss her." I'd think "Yuck no way, what an abomination!! Never!" I would begin to pray, not because I was tempted, but because I *knew* it was the voice of the enemy satan. He is a liar and a destroyer of anyone who will listen to and believe the lies. I didn't believe the lies, because I *know who I am*. I am not homosexual, nor ever will be. I love that a man is strength and comfort and it doesn't hurt that they possess parts that fit mine beautifully. Enough said on that, you know what I mean. I am thankful God made me a female. I would not trade heaven and a wholeness and peace in my mind and soul for anything.

You must know the enemy has a voice. It <u>isn't</u> yours!!! You have an enemy. Know his tactics. Know his tricks. When you do, **you can overcome any and all of his schemes against you.** He won't give up until you keep denouncing him and his lies. Only when you open up your heart to God, seek His directions through scripture and follow His ways will you be able to ***withstand the devil.*** Each time I prayed, I felt stronger in my convictions and the voice stopped altogether. Thankfully, it hasn't happened since. So I asked God, "Why did you put me through that knowing I was heterosexual?" He said "So that you would understand how many people get involved with same sex relationships. They believe that if they *hear* it in their own minds, it must be truth. And if the voice keeps on telling them over and over again, it must also be true. Only, they are wrong. It is a lie from the enemy to destroy them and keep them from Me." He said that all sexual sin is the same, whether it is fornication, adultery or homosexuality. It is all the same to Him; a deception of the truth, a deviation of His created pure sexuality which He made in each man and woman.

Think this through, He made each sex, male and female with certain sexual parts that complement each other. We even name mechanical parts male and female, since they are put together the same way. The Lord told me to tell you this, so that even if one of you reading this understands, becomes healed and delivered, it was worth sharing with you. I am not afraid to tell you this since God told me to share what I learned from Him. I *asked* God to *show me*. Jesus was tempted in all ways and yet without sin. As for those of you who were tempted or have fallen into this type of sexual deviation from God's plan, know that He loves you and wants you to come back. His plan is loving, caring and fulfilling of your destiny and wholeness of mind, soul and spirit. Please give God a chance to show you His plan before you just turn away. Let go of everything you think you need and desire for a higher, greater, healthier lifestyle in HIM. No sin has overcome you that cannot be forgiven. (See Appendix under Lingerie for recommended reading)

Your hope and salvation is in HIM and through HIM, in all things pertaining to life. He is waiting for you to see how much He loves you and will do all that is needed to keep you from any and all sin, if you are willing to follow Him and obey His words. He ***is*** the word and the word is **Him**. Trust Him to do His best work on your behalf. He hasn't left you, did you leave Him? He wants you back. He gave up His one and only Son for you. Would you give up your child for someone? Even after all I have been through, I can't say I would, but if it would save another child and I knew mine would go to heaven, all I can say is it would hurt like heck but I might do it. That is how precious you are to HIM and me as well.

Maybe you were told you should have the freedom to choose for yourself and live your life your own way. Maybe you were molested by same sex offenders. Don't let sexual, emotional ties keep you bound up. I hope this scripture helps in your understanding:

2 Peter 2:19, 20
"While they (the world) promise them liberty,
they themselves are the *servants* of corruption:
for of whom a man is overcome, **of the same is he brought into bondage**.
For *if after they have escaped the pollutions of the world* **through the knowledge of the Lord and Savior Jesus Christ,** they are **again entangled therein**, and overcome, the latter end is worse with them than the beginning."

Find freedom now and let Him heal your wounded heart and soul. Take time to allow His word to renew your mind and soul and refresh your new life in Him. We get our greatest victories from our greatest struggles. Keep on in faith no matter what the enemy says. Remember the enemy not only wants hostages, he prefers there are no living survivors. My prayer for you is healing, a peaceful loving relationship with God and for you to have a beautiful ever after. Think of who you will bless and help heal by your testimony. No one person, kept to themselves, accomplishes much, but if that same one person shares what they know and have learned to just one person and they share it, it will spread and heal more people. Know that you are loved and not judged.

It is love that compels me to write this to you, risking ridicule myself for sharing my experience, knowing it may be taken wrong. You are worth the risk.

Closet purging time for, Lingerie

It is not a simple thing to make decisions about our own sexuality these days. Hopefully I have given you enough information to do so. It's my prayer you will find a good church to assist you in making changes to your lifestyle towards a godly healthy life.

Looking deeper yet into your closet, what secret sexual things are you ashamed to say you have? Is there anything that promotes same sex relationships or adultery or sex without marriage? Remove anything that will encourage, tempt or shame you if you keep it. Remember, this sexual life that God made is for oneness in a relationship, not to destroy our morals, our character or our self-worth. It shouldn't bring pain, physically or emotional to either partner. Remove the unfit, unhealthy sexual garments, and exchange them for the rich robes of God. ***He wants to clothe you with His Love***. His love endures and gives us courage to love ourselves first and then others.

Journal page for chapter twenty-three, Lingerie

If you have already opened your gift of purity, meaning virginity, before marriage I want you to know that God does forgive our past decisions and actions. However, we can't keep in those unhealthy sexual lifestyles and serve God at the same time.

Please do be honest. You may feel ashamed to write down what your past sexual experiences are but do so on another paper and as you list those down, compare what the scriptures say about those sexual practices. After you write them down, pray over it and then ask God to forgive you of any sexual sin. He is faithful to forgive. Release all your needs, sexual and emotional, to Him. Remember He created you a sexual being. He knows all about your needs and wants as a woman. Then write down your dreams for a healthy God blessed relationship here on this page. Our goals are to become whole and healthy and happier women who serve and love God. It doesn't mean we become frigid or neglectful of our sexuality. It just has to have order to it. Go ahead and burn that paper after you have given your past sins and painful experiences to God. You are now a new creature in Christ, He gives you a new day to begin all over again. Choose Him and His path and you will find freedom from all things. Nothing is too hard for the Lord, nothing.

Mirror, Mirror

After reading and working through the previous chapters, I hope you have a good idea of what you have been carrying around. It has been weeks and or months of hard work for you as you went through both your emotional and physical closets. I hope you were able to get some closure and relief from your past baggage. When I started acknowledging that I had value as a human being, I began to look at myself differently. I dressed differently, acted differently, spoke more positively and I avoided those who may be in a position to hurt me further. I had to see value in myself first, and then others valued me. I am a more confident person today, not because of my outer appearance, but because of the inner healing God gave me. I am a work in progress just like you are.

Hebrews 10:35
"Do not cast away your confidence, which has a great reward."

When we first look in the mirror with pain, we see only darkness and feel an inner void. When we unload our burdens on Christ, we can begin to see the light. When we take positive actions for our future, it lifts the fog of lies and we see hope in the mirror of life. Others have seen our lives changing in these last few months. We become a benefit to others when we share how He changed us and how He walked us through the hard times. When we reach our destiny, our God-given vocation, we will shine for all to see. We will be so blessed that it will pour out like water to a dry and thirsty land. After a while, we should mirror Christ's life, so that when others see us they also see Him *in us*.

When you look in the mirror today, what do you see? Can you finally agree with God when He says you are wonderfully made? God has never given up on you and He never will. We have not yet fully arrived, but we are in the process of becoming princesses, the daughters of The King. Someone once told me to "fake it till I make it." I am not a good faker. However, in this instance, I have to say it is a good idea. ***Put on those princess gowns***. It is not pretending, it is ***fulfilling*** your destiny. It may be overwhelming, but it is our destiny to be the daughters of God. The process takes time and strength, direction, support and motivation. I hope I have given you some of those for the rest of your journey. Remember when I asked you to take a "before" picture? That was so you could see the physical change in yourself, after you finished the book. Maybe you have lost weight. Maybe you stand taller, have a new job or have started new relationships. If you did the purging, at the very least, your closets should be cleaner. I know mine are physically and spiritually as well. I can breathe easier now, no dust.

Then I asked you to do a makeover. Did you do that? That was so you could explore new things and get out of your comfort zone. Did you try on new and different garments too?

We get stuck in a rut with our lives and need a jump-start to get us thinking outside the box. Have you had more compliments? I want you to see yourself, as you really are, the beloved of the King. You are the fiancé to the best *groom* Jesus. You are worthy of love and kindness and all that is good.

We also need to look in the mirror of our souls and make some decisions about where we go from here. After all is said and done, what changes have you made spiritually throughout this book? What does your spiritual life reflect in the mirror now? What changes will you continue to make in the future towards your destiny? Which final destination will be yours? If after reading the whole book, it would be sad if you didn't make any changes that were long lasting. I hope you don't forget your journey through this book, or the lessons in it.

James 1:23, 24
"For if any be a hearer of the word, and not a doer,
he is like unto a man beholding his natural face in a glass (mirror):
For he beholds himself, and goes his way,
and straightway *forgets* what manner of man he was."

1 Corinthians 13:12
"For now we see through a glass, darkly; but then face to face:
now I know in part; but then shall I know even as also I am known."

We know little this side of Heaven, but when we get to the other side all will be revealed and made known. In the beginning of this journey we didn't see well. We couldn't see God, but now, having a relationship with Him, we see and in Heaven we will see Him face to face. We knew little of ourselves before and now we know we were created with our own destiny.

Here's a new Quote from me to you:

"Refusing to follow others' paths means:
God designed a plan that is as unique as you are.
You no longer have to compete, compare or even compromise.
Enjoy the freedom that brings to all of us."

Journal page for chapter twenty four,
Mirror, Mirror

Take a new look in the mirror. Take your time, look deeply. Who do you see before you now? Take a new photo of yourself today. Note the differences. What life changes have occurred during your journey with me and this book? What new opportunities has God opened up for you? Are you ready for travel? Are your suitcases also empty of all negative clothing, both physical and spiritual? What are you committed to do to continue your journey of healing?

Appendix

This section is for those who want to know more information on selected chapters as follows:

Shoes:

The warriors in Bible times shod their feet with sandals that had sharp metal like nails embedded in the sole of their shoes. It enabled them to get away quickly and not get stuck in the terrain if it was slippery. They would also use the shoes as a weapon to stomp hard on the enemy's foot or leg or such. The straps went all the way up to the ankle so it wouldn't shift or slip off as they ran. The straps were closely woven from side to side across the top so the stones wouldn't get thru.

Dancing Clothes:

Here are some more scriptures on joy.

Psalms 15:11

But let all those that put their trust in thee—rejoice: let them ever shout for joy, *because thou defends them*: let them also that love thy name *be joyful in thee.*

Psalms 16:11

You will show me the path of life: *in Your (God's) presence is fullness of joy*; at Your right hand there are pleasures for evermore.

Psalms 27:6

And now shall *my head be lifted up above mine enemies* round about me: therefore will I offer in his tabernacle sacrifices of joy; I will sing, yea, I will sing praises unto the Lord.

Psalms 51:8

Make me to hear joy and gladness; that the bones, which thou hast broken, may rejoice.

You are a gift:

More scriptures on gifts from the Bible.

James 1:17

"Every good and perfect gift is from above, and comes down from the Father of Lights, with whom there is no variation or shadow of turning. Of His own free will He brought us forth by the word of truth, that we might be a kind of first fruits of His creatures."

Romans chapter 12:6-8

"Having then *gifts* differing according to the grace that is given to us, let us use them: if <u>prophecy</u>, let us prophesy in proportion to our faith, Or <u>ministry</u>, let us use it in our ministering, He who <u>teaches</u>, in teaching, He who <u>exhorts</u>, in exhortation, he who <u>gives</u> with liberality, he who <u>leads</u>, with diligence, he who shows <u>mercy</u>, with cheerfulness."

2 Timothy 1; 6, 7

"Therefore I remind you to stir up *the gift* of God which is in you through the laying on of my hands. For God has not given us a spirit of fear, but of power and of love and of a sound mind."

Your Glorious Destiny:

Here is the whole scripture for those who don't have a bible.

Proverbs 31:10-31

Who can find a virtuous woman? For her price is far above rubies.

The heart of her husband doth safely trust in her, so that he shall have no need of spoil.

She will do him good and not evil all the days of her life.

She seeks wool, and flax, and works willingly with her hands.

She is like the merchants' ships; she brings her food from afar.

She rises while it is yet night, gives meat to her household, and a portion to her maidens.

She considers a field, and buys it: with the fruit of her hands she plants a vineyard.

She girds her loins with strength, and strengthens her arms.

She perceives that her merchandise is good: her candle goes not out by night.

She lays her hands to the spindle, and her hands hold the distaff.

She stretches out her hand to the poor; yea, she reaches forth her hands to the needy.

She is not afraid of the snow for her household are clothed with scarlet.

She makes herself coverings of tapestry; her clothing *is* silk and purple.

Her husband is known in the gates, when he sits among the elders of the land.

She makes fine linen, and sells it; and delivers girdles unto the merchant.

Strength and honor are her clothing; and she shall rejoice in time to come.

She opens her mouth with wisdom; and in her tongue is the law of kindness.

She looks well to the ways of her household, and eats not the bread of idleness.

Her children arise up, and call her blessed; her husband also, and he praises her.

Many daughters have done virtuously, but thou excels them all.

Favor is deceitful, and beauty is vain: but a woman that fears the LORD, she shall be praised.

Give her of the fruit of her hands; and let her own works praise her in the gates."

What is Salvation and why do I need it?

Let's go back to the beginning of Creation, God created mankind for his companionship and our benefit. He let us have free will and Adam and Eve sinned by disobeying God. He told them not to eat from the tree of "***Knowledge of good and evil***". They already had "good." God had created everything they needed, not only for survival but also for a completely wonderful life, including eternity with God, all that was good and loving. What they did not understand was that the only thing God kept *from* them was evil. Therefore, when satan deceived Eve, she thought God was holding out on them. *What more good was God keeping from them?* Nothing. He was *withholding evil and its bondage to sin, and its destructive selfish nature.* Adam and Eve were not exposed to sin or evil before satan came to the earth. So they ate and became separated from eternal life and from the perfect life with God.

Actually, **the first garment ever made** was made by God to cover their now felt nakedness. God was the very first clothing designer. He sacrificed one of his own creations, an animal that was blameless, spilling its blood for a spiritual sacrificial propitiation for sin. The definition of propitiation is to fulfill or satisfy sins punishment. It must have hurt God to kill his own creation. It was the first blood sacrifice. God kept on lovingly providing for them, first for their fleshly needs and then their spiritual ones.

Throughout Jewish history, they have used animal sacrifices to cover sins. The priests had to use a pure, blameless and spotless animal. The priest would hold the ram's head and put the sins on the animal, then it was killed in a certain way. That animal took the punishment for people's sins with its life.

Now, many years passed by and multitudes of people sinned and rebelled against God, creating new gods they wanted to serve. God sent a punishing flood to eliminate all the sin-filled people. God regretted that, and sent a rainbow to show us He would make a promise to never again flood the earth and kill all of humankind. The people still rebelled. God has seen it all. There is no new sin, just the same rebellious spirit. Therefore, God decided he would send many prophets throughout the years to tell those He loved, "Repent, turn from your sins and be healed." That worked for a while but then satan, being unleashed on earth, kept tempting the people and getting them to believe lies about God and about real life. *His lies are so clever and so believable that even some true followers of God will follow them.*

Therefore, God decided to send His one and only begotten Son, Jesus, who set aside His own royal garments to come down to earth and wear our earthly wardrobe. God sent Jesus to be born of a woman. Not just any woman, a virgin. She was pure and her heart was towards God. Today we would call her a spirit-filled believer. She heard the word of God in her life and followed it. The Holy Spirit came upon her and she conceived Jesus, who was God and man. She gave birth in obedience, thus fulfilling her destiny.

As a child, Jesus grew strong in spirit, filled with wisdom, and the grace of God was with him. At age twelve, he asked many questions of the temple teachers. When He was thirty years old, He was baptized by John the Baptist, filled with the Holy Spirit upon his baptism. Forty days and nights Jesus was tempted by the devil. In rebuking these temptations, Jesus proved that **using the word of God and being full of the Holy Spirit,** we, like him**, could live a purer life with God's assistance.**

Jesus, calling himself God, angered the priests and elders and they, being envious, sought to kill him. He fulfilled the Old Testament prophesies which told that there would be a coming Savior. Jesus accepted the cross, the most humiliating death at that time. Those of us who were humiliated by abuse have that in common with Jesus. He was humiliated for our redemption. We were humiliated and yes, we too can overcome the enemy, just as Christ did. He was beaten, verbally abused, enduring it all the time and keeping the focus of his mission for our souls, then returning to His father—God. **This life is our journey back to God.** Your life on this earth is only temporary. Eternity in heaven or hell, *by our own decision* is forever. When Jesus died, he fulfilled the Old Testament prophesies. He provided himself as the sacrificial blood shed for all sins forever. He was raised from the dead to conquer death and the bondage that sin has over us. Satan no longer has authority on us when we choose God's salvation plan for us through Jesus Christ's bloodshed for our sins.

Once again, God provided for us. He knew that we were going to miss Jesus being with us. We would miss his words, healing and godly counsel, so He sent the Holy Spirit to be that for us. In Matthew, the Holy Spirit is the one who overcame Mary and she became pregnant. The Holy Spirit came upon Jesus after John the Baptist baptized Him. The Holy Spirit made himself known through the disciples at Pentecost as they spoke in other languages. He was and still is part of the Trinity of God: God the father, God the Son Jesus, God the Holy Spirit. Unfortunately, many still reject the Holy Spirit, and when they do, they reject God who sent him.

Jesus said in Matthew 12:31, 32
"Wherefore I say unto you, all manner of sin and blasphemy shall be forgiven
unto men: but the blasphemy against the Holy Ghost shall not be forgiven unto men.
And whosoever speaks a word against the Son of man, it shall be forgiven
Him: but whosoever speaks against the Holy Ghost, it shall not be forgiven him,
neither in this world, neither in the world to come."

Lingerie:

If you want to know how or why other openly gay/homosexuals have found freedom and fulfillment in Christ, I recommended reading these books.

Out from a far place, by Christopher Yaon

Secret Thoughts of an Unlikely Convert, by Rosaria Butterfield

About the Author

Laurie is known for her communication skills, her love of people and genuine concern for others. She loves the outdoors and walking. Her God –given ability for design and visual detail have helped her create things that others can enjoy. She has painted a collection of paintings depicting her journey of healing. Hoping to show them in public as awareness and meaningful contemplation. She is currently working on a new book, "Lot's Wife, could her name be Martha?"

Heavenly Adoption Paper

I, the undersigned, do herein this day agree to be adopted by my Heavenly Father, God. I have willingly denounced my past life of sin and wish to begin a new life with Jesus Christ. I accept the position as a daughter of the Most High God, a princess in the kingdom of my future home, heaven. I understand this is a permanent position and that God will not leave me nor forsake me, as I am now one of his children, forever. He promises to take care of all my needs. I accept His divine destiny for my life.

Signed, _____

On this day _____

In the year of our Lord, _____